The Hidden Places of
SUSSEX

By
Emma Roberts

© Travel Publishing Ltd.

Published by:
Travel Publishing Ltd
7a Apollo House, Calleva Park
Aldermaston, Berks, RG7 8TN

ISBN 1-902-00780-8
© Travel Publishing Ltd

First Published:	*1989*	*Fourth Edition:*	*2000*
Second Edition:	*1996*	*Fifth Edition:*	*2002*
Third Edition:	*1998*		

HIDDEN PLACES REGIONAL TITLES

Cambs & Lincolnshire	Chilterns
Cornwall	Derbyshire
Devon	Dorset, Hants & Isle of Wight
East Anglia	Gloucestershire, Wiltshire & Somerset
Heart of England	Hereford, Worcs & Shropshire
Highlands & Islands	Kent
Lake District & Cumbria	Lancashire & Cheshire
Lincolnshire & Nottinghamshire	Northumberland & Durham
Somerset	Sussex
Thames Valley	Yorkshire

HIDDEN PLACES NATIONAL TITLES

England	Ireland
Scotland	Wales

Printing by: Scotprint, Haddington

Maps by: © Maps in Minutes ™ (2002) © Crown Copyright, Ordnance Survey 2002

Editor: Emma Roberts

Cover Design: Lines & Words, Aldermaston

Cover Photographs: Chalk Cliffs near Beachy Head; Alfriston on the South Downs; "Batemans" near Burwash © www.britainonview.com

Text Photographs: © www.britainonview.com

Foreword

The Hidden Places is a collection of easy to use travel guides taking you in this instance, on a relaxed but informative tour of the county of Sussex, a county rich in heritage and endowed with attractive rolling hills and beautiful woodlands which contain a wealth of delightful rural hamlets and villages. The charming and picturesque coastline is steeped in the history of the Battle of Hastings and the Cinque Ports but also possesses some delightful seaside towns. The county is packed with historical sites from the Roman town of Chichester and the 11th Century Arundel Castle to the Tudor Ruins of Cowdray Park and the grand old houses such as the Elizabethan Wakehurst Place. Sussex is equally famous for great names from the world of arts that include HG Wells, Anthony Trollope, Virginia Wolf and Rudyard Kipling. Sussex is definitely a county worth exploring!

This edition of *The Hidden Places of Sussex* is published *in full colour.* All *Hidden Places* titles are now published in colour which ensures that readers can properly appreciate the attractive scenery and impressive places of interest in the county and, of course, in the rest of the British Isles. We do hope that you like the new format.

Our books contain a wealth of interesting information on the history, the countryside, the towns and villages and the more established places of interest. But they also promote the more secluded and little known visitor attractions and places to stay, eat and drink many of which are easy to miss unless you know exactly where you are going.

We include various types of accommodation, restaurants, public houses, teashops, historic houses, museums, and many other attractions throughout the county, all of which are comprehensively indexed. Most places are accompanied by an attractive photograph and are easily located by using the map at the beginning of each chapter. We do not award merit marks or rankings but concentrate on describing the more interesting, unusual or unique features of each place with the aim of making the reader's stay in the local area an enjoyable and stimulating experience.

Whether you are visiting the area for business or pleasure or in fact are living in the county we do hope that you enjoy reading and using this book. We are always interested in what readers think of places covered (or not covered) in our guides so please do not hesitate to use the reader reaction forms provided to give us your considered comments. We also welcome any general comments which will help us improve the guides themselves. Finally if you are planning to visit any other corner of the British Isles we would like to refer you to the list of other Travel Publishing titles to be found at the rear of the book and to the Travel Publishing website at www.travelpublishing.co.uk.

Travel Publishing

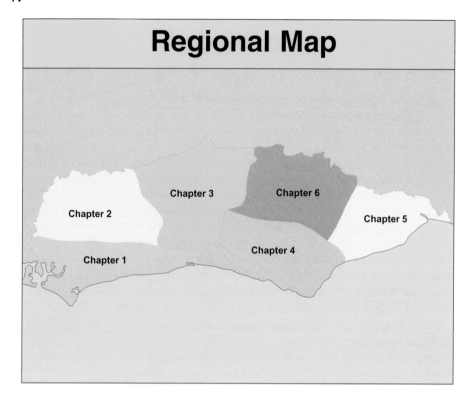

Contents

1 Chichester and the West Sussex Coast

This western, coastal region of West Sussex is centred around Chichester, the county town, Arundel, with its magnificent castle, and the resorts of Littlehampton, Bognor

River Arun, West Sussex

Regis and Worthing. An ecclesiastical centre for over 900 years, Chichester was founded by the Romans in the 1ST century. Its fine, natural harbour, once a busy place for trade and also smugglers, is now a lively yachting centre with delightful old fishing villages found along its many inlets. Nearby, at Fishbourne, the Roman conquerors built a splendid palace for the Celtic King Cogidubnus who collaborated with the invaders. The largest estate north of the Alps, the Roman remains at Fishbourne were only uncovered this century whilst a new water mains was being installed.

The inland town of Arundel is not only home to an impressive castle situated beside the River Arun but also the area's second cathedral. Built by the Roman Catholic family living at the castle, Arundel Cathedral is famous for its Corpus Christi Festival.

Back to the coast and the bustling resorts of Littlehampton, Bognor Regis and Worthing. Overshadowed by their great rival to the east - Brighton - each one of these former fishing villages has much to offer in a modest and

Arundel

timeless manner. Finally, the small town of Selsey together with the island of Selsey Bill - the most southwesterly tip of West Sussex, is a charming place full of history and pleasant walks along the coastline.

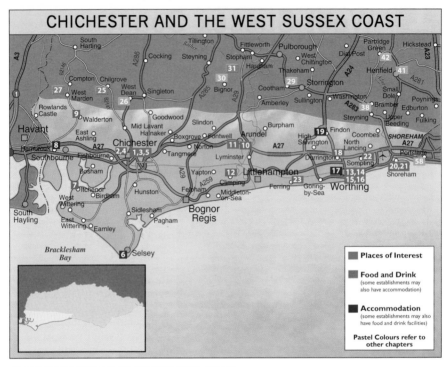

PLACES TO STAY, EAT, DRINK AND SHOP

CHICHESTER

Set on the low lying plain between the south coast and the South Downs, Chichester, the county town of West Sussex, was founded by the Romans in the 1ST century. The invading Roman legions used the town as a base camp, christening it *Noviomagus*, "the new city of the plain", and both the city walls and the four major thoroughfares - North, South, East and West Streets - follow the original Roman town plan. They cross at the point where a fine 16TH century **Butter Cross** now stands; an ornate structure built in 1500 by Bishop Edward Story to provide shelter for the many traders who came to sell their wares at the busy market.

The city walls, originally consisting of raised earthwork embankments built in an irregular 11-sided shape, were constructed

Chichester Butter Cross

around AD 200. Over the subsequent centuries alterations and improvements were made and, today, the remaining walls mainly date from medieval times and large sections still form the boundary between the old and new city. A stroll along the circular Walls Walk provides an informative view of the city's two thousand years of heritage. After the Romans left, the Saxons came, in AD 500, and Chichester's modern name is derived from Cissa's ceaster after the Saxon King Cissa.

Chichester also has a long and colourful ecclesiastical history and, although St Wilfrid chose nearby Selsey as the site of the area's first cathedral, the conquering Normans, who moved all country bishoprics to towns, built a new cathedral on the present site in the late 11TH century. Resting on Roman foundations, the construction work began in 1091 and the finished building was finally consecrated in 1184. A fire, just three years later, all but destroyed the cathedral and a rebuilding programme was started by Richard of Chichester in the 13TH century. A venerated bishop who was canonised in 1262, Richard of Chichester was subsequently adopted as the city's patron saint.

Lying in the heart of the city, **Chichester Cathedral** (see panel on page 4), a centre for Christian worship for over 900 years, is unique on two counts. Firstly, it is the only medieval English cathedral that can be seen from the sea rather than being secluded by its own close and, secondly, it has a detached belfry. The existing tower was thought not to have been sturdy enough to take the cathedral bells and hence another separate building was needed. Indeed, in 1861, the cathedral spire blew down in a storm and demolished a large section of the nave. The present 277 foot spire was designed by

CHICHESTER CATHEDRAL

West Street, Chichester, West Sussex, PO19 1PX
Tel: 01243 782595 Fax: 01243 536190
e-mail: vo@chicath.freeserve.co.uk
website: www.chichester-cathedral.org.uk

Chichester's Cathedral, rich in history, architecture, music and art, provides the focus for any visit to the city. Guided tours are available whilst, the splendid Cathedral Precinct and the delightful Bishop's Garden are also open to the public and a joy to explore. The children's education centre offers special childrens tours and activities linked to the school National Curriculum. Situated next to the main shopping area and within walking distance of other notable attractions, it is possible to combine a visit to the Cathedral with other venues such as Pallant House Art Gallery or Chichester Festival Theatre. For shoppers it's an easy matter to take a break, pop into the Cathedral Bell Rooms restaurant for morning coffee, afternoon tea or a full meal, then resume shopping. In the summer visitors can sit in the tranquil walled garden and admire the splendour of the Cathedral and surrounding buildings. In the detached 15th century Bell Tower is the Cathedral gift shop where guide books, postcards, souvenirs and gifts may be purchased.

Visitors are very welcome to join with the congregation in acts of worship. Evensong at 5.30pm

each evening (3.30 pm on Sundays) is when the renowned Cathedral Choir, with its ley vicars and boy choristers can be heard on most days. Visitors are also welcome to the Sung Eucharist at 11am on Sunday and to join the community for a cup of coffee afterwards.

One of the great features of Chichester Cathedral is the use of modern works of art to invigorate and beautify the Cathedral. Paintings, stained glass, tapestries and embroideries have all been employed. Look out in particular for the painting of 'The Baptism of Christ' by Hans Feibusch (1951), Graham Sutherland's ' Noli me Tangere' from 1960 and Patrick Procktor's stunning ' Baptism' from 1984. Marc Chagall's 1978 stained glass window should not be missed. Based on the theme of Psalm 150 '...let everything that hath breath praise the Lord', it is one of the finest examples of its type from the late 20th century. There's a tapestry by John Piper, completed in 1966, as a reredos to the high altar and another, from 1985, by Ursula Benker-Schirmer in the retro-choir. Behind the Bishop's throne is a magnificent embroidered panel designed by Joan Freeman in 1993. Also worth a close look are the

sculptures, Virgin and Child from 1988, by John Skelton and Christ in Judgement executed by Philip Jackson ten years later. Don't miss Skelton's polished polyphant stone and beaten copper font from 1983. Outside, by the bell tower, is an impressive statue in bronze of St. Richard by Philip Jackson.

All these are set in an ancient building that has stood here from Norman times. It was destroyed by fire in 1114 and the present building and additions date from then. The Cathedral suffered from years of neglect but since the mid 19th century a continuing programme of restoration has been taking place.

A great deal has been achieved in recent years to ensure that the structure of the Cathedral is in good order. The interior stonework has been thoroughly cleaned, the ceilings restored and their beauty enhanced by the installation of up-lighting. Among the many early features worth looking at are the 12th century Chichester Reliefs, two carved stone panels depicting part of the story of the raising of Lazarus, and a collection of 16th century paintings by Lambert Barnard of past bishops and the Kings and Queens of England.

Guided Tours: am and pm Easter to end of October. For special arrangements and group bookings, contact the booking officer. For children's and educational visits, contact the education officer.

Sir Gilbert Scott and, in keeping with the building's original style, it can also be seen for miles around from all directions.

Among the treasures within the cathedral is the Shrine of St Richard of Chichester along with some fine Norman arches, a set of 14TH century choir stalls and, surprisingly, some excellent modern works of art. There is also an altar tapestry by John Piper, a stained glass window by Marc Chagall and a painting by Graham Sutherland of Christ appearing to Mary Magdalene. However, the most important treasures to be seen are the Norman sculptures: *The Raising of Lazarus* and *Christ Arriving in Bethany* which can be found on the south wall. The **Prebendal School**, the cathedral choir school, is the oldest school in Sussex and it stands alongside the main building.

From the Middle Ages until the 18TH century, Chichester was a major trading and exporting centre for the Sussex woollen trade and some handsome merchants' houses were built using these profits. The city's oldest building is St Mary's Hospital, dating from the 13TH century, which was established to house the deserving elderly of Chichester.

The almshouses that were built into the hospital walls are still inhabited and the chapel has some unique misericords. The city's **Guildhall**, built around 1282 as the church of the Franciscans, is a Grade I listed building. Later becoming Chichester's town hall and law courts, it was here in 1804, that the poet William Blake was tried for treason and acquitted. Today, it is home to a display telling the story of the building and the surrounding Priory Park in which it stands.

There are also some fine Georgian buildings to be found in the city and, in the area known as The Pallants, lies the elegant **Pallant House**. A splendid example of a red brick town house, it was

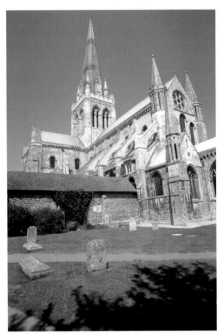

Chichester Cathedral

built in 1712 by the local wine merchant Henry 'Lisbon' Peckham and the building is guarded by a wonderful pair of carved stone dodos, which have given rise to its local nickname - the Dodo House. Another curious feature is the observation tower on the house, from which Peckham would look out for his merchant ships returning laden with goods from the Iberian Peninsula. Today, the house is the Pallant House Gallery, one of the country's finest galleries outside London, and home to a modern art collection that includes works by Moore, Sikert, Piper, Picasso and Cèzanne.

One of the Chichester's most distinctive modern buildings can be found at Oaklands Park, close by the city walls. The **Chichester Festival Theatre** was opened in 1962 and the splendid hexagonal building has since gained a reputation for

THE CHEQUERS INN

203 Oving Road, Chichester,
West Sussex, PO19 4ER
Tel: 01423 786427

An unusually shaped white building located on a main road on the outskirts of Chichester town centre, **The Chequers Inn** is run by Annette and her partner Danny, both from East Sussex and both full of enthusiasm for transforming The Chequers into a 'super pub'! An open-plan, simply decorated interior is well lit and makes a cheery venue for the loyal crowd of locals and the members of the pool and darts teams that regularly compete in local league competitions. This is a real community pub with a genuinely warm spirit and lively atmosphere.

In addition to the picnic tables and umbrellas out front, there's a sizeable garden at the rear with seating in between the many trees and shrubs, making an appealing green retreat to relax and catch some sun away from the hustle and bustle of the town centre. Annette is a champion of real ales, and there's always an excellent selection on offer from the long line up of pumps. Food tends to be light bar snacks and freshly made sandwiches, but the kitchen can stretch to a few plates of chips when asked! At the time of going to print, bed and breakfast accommodation was under negotiation.

staging the outstanding classical and contemporary drama, opera and ballet. A focal point of the annual Chichester Festival, along with the cathedral, for two weeks during July when the city is alive with a myriad of cultural events.

The **Mechanical Music and Doll Collection** (see panel below) is one of the city's more unusual museums and represents a fascinating walk through the last 100 years of mechanical music. Playing the tunes of late 19TH century public houses through to genteel Victorian parlour songs, the beautifully

MECHANICAL MUSIC AND DOLL COLLECTION

Church Road, Portfield, Chichester, West Sussex PO19 4HN
Tel: 01243 372646 Fax: 01243 370299

In a former Victorian church, a mile to the east of Chichester city centre, can be found this magical collection of mechanical musical instruments. There are musical boxes, barrel pianos, organs etc. and on Wednesday afternoons in the summer visitors have the chance to hear them. Listen to the lively music of the Victor-ian parlours, streets and pubs, and the glorious sounds of orchestrions that filled the dance halls in the twenties. You can even take groups there by appointment for a tour any time throughout the year. Children adore these music machines, and adults sometimes remember the tunes!

restored instruments are put through their paces on a regular basis. Also to be seen within the collection are Edison phonographs, early horned gramophones, stereoscopic viewers and over 100 dolls spanning the years from 1830 to 1930.

Housed in an 18TH century corn store, **Chichester District Museum** explores local history through displays and hands-on activities. The journey starts back through time when visitors can find out about local geology and prehistory, including Boxgrove Man. Life in Roman, Saxon and medieval Chichester can also be discovered. The journey continues with displays on Chichester during the Civil War, and visitors can see how the city changed during Georgian and Victorian times including displays on the market. The story is brought up to date with information about Chichester post 1900. The museum has a programme of changing exhibitions and there are a wide range of events including talks and walks.

Located in the Barracks, the **Royal Military Police Museum** (see panel on page 8) traces military police history from Tudor times to present day operations with artefacts from various conflicts over the centuries including a nostalgic National Service kit layout.

Chichester is also now home to one of the largest planetariums in Britain – the **South Downs Planetarium**. A purely educational establishment, it is housed on the site of the boys' high school and only open to the public for specific shows.

Once a busy port, the city is now a haven for all boat lovers and yachtsmen, with a bustling harbour from which there are boat trips, and around 12,000 resident boats and some fabulous yachts moored in one of Europe's largest marinas. A particularly pleasant waterside walk can be taken from the city's impressive canal basin, along the four mile stretch of

THE WOOL PACK INN

71 Fishbourne Road, Chichester,
West Sussex PO19 3JJ
Tel: 01243 785707 Fax: 01243 839935
e-mail: woolpackboss@aol.com
website: www.woolpackinn.net

Roger and his wife Julie Jackson have developed **The Wool Pack Inn** during the four years that they have been tenants there and built up a loyal following of regulars. Situated on the 'old' A27 to Pompery, just on the outskirts of Chichester, this busy pub is housed in a relatively modern and substantial brick building, with ten tastefully furnished rooms currently being finished in a separate building to the side.

The accommodation is aimed at corporates during the week and discerning tourists over the weekends. There's also an accessible room for disabled guests located on the ground floor. Inside, the open plan pub is smartly decorated with a shiny wood ceiling, classic wood panelling and a bright colour scheme of contrasting primary colours. A smattering of comfy leather drawing room chairs, sofas and candelabras add to the scene. French windows lead out onto a patio and sizeable, tree rimmed lawn for al fresco eating and drinking. Julie looks after the smooth running of the kitchen along with her efficient team of staff, and conjures up an interesting range of home made snacks and a la carte menus, which include handmade cheeses and Jersey ice cream.

Chichester Canal (all that now remains of a once longer waterway from Arundel to Portsmouth), to Chichester Harbour. The canal opened in 1822, taking vessels of up to 150 tons principally carrying coal. The last commercial cargo travelled the route in 1928 but, following restoration work it is now a delightful walk, and if you're feeling weary there is a cruise boat on which to make the return journey.

ROYAL MILITARY POLICE MUSEUM

The Keep, Roussillon Barracks, Chichester, West Sussex, PO19 6BL
Tel: 01243 534225 Fax: 01243 534288
e-mail: museum@rhqrmp.freeserve.co.uk
website: www.rmpmuseum.org.uk

This is an essential visit for anyone interested in military history and a fascinating insight into the history and workings of the **Royal Military Police** for anyone else. Established in 1979, the present museum was formally opened in 1985 and has full registration with the Museums and Galleries Commission. Military Police, also known as redcaps because of their distinctive headgear, have been around for a long time. Walking through the various fascinating exhibits, it is possible to trace their entire history from Tudor times to the recent conflicts in the former Yugoslavia. Display cases contain life size models of military policemen dressed in the varieties of uniforms they have used at different times and at different points of the globe. Everything is there from full camouflage combat gear to the dress uniform worn by a mounted officer at a ceremonial occasion. Also included are maps, weapons and communications equipment the corps have used in their various theatres of operations.

Visitors can try on some of the uniforms, have their fingerprints taken and learn about the diverse role of the military police. A .22 palm pistol is part of a haul of weapons confiscated during the RMP operations, aimed at reducing weapon holding, in Republica Serbska during 1996-97. This murderous little device is lethal at close quarters and easily concealed. From the period at the end of WWII is a complicated looking illicit still recovered from a displaced persons camp in Hamburg, 1946. From the same period is the Walther P38 pistol used in the murder of Sergeant Southcott. He and two others arrested Teofil Walasek on charges of murder, rape and robbery. When they apprehended him at the railway station he was searched but they neglected to check his overcoat. Back at HQ Walasek produced the pistol, killed Southcott, wounded two others and escaped but was later recaptured and sentenced to death.

Amongst the exhibits is a ferret armoured car of the type used extensively by the Redcaps in anti-terrorist operations in Cyprus and Malaya during the 1950s. This one, which sits outside the museum, is in the livery of 17 Ghurkha Division Provost Company and was crewed entirely by RMP NCOs providing close escort to the general officer commanding the division during road moves. A BSA motorcycle was in use from 1939-1964. Many modern exhibits are on display from theatres of operations ranging from Northern Ireland to Bosnia and Kosovo. The Northern Ireland exhibits include captured terrorist weapons, commercially and home-made, uniform items and accounts of incidents in which the RMP were involved. Outside the building are two imposing statues of Military Policemen, one standing at ease upon a large block the other on horseback. In the purpose built Broakes Room is a comprehensive collection of medals awarded to members of the RMP over the years of its existence.

AROUND CHICHESTER

MID LAVANT
2 miles N of Chichester on the A286

This attractive village, along with its neighbour East Lavant, is named after the small river which flows from Singleton into Chichester Harbour. There are spectacular views from here northwards over the South Downs, which it is said provided the inspiration for the words 'England's Green and Pleasant Land' which appear in William Blake's famous poem, *Jerusalem*.

GOODWOOD
3 miles NE of Chichester off the A285

This is not a village but the spectacular, flint embossed country home of the Dukes of Richmond for the past 300 years - **Goodwood House** - that was first acquired by the 1ST Duke of Richmond (the natural son of Charles II and his beautiful French mistress, Louise de Keroualle) in 1697 so that he could ride with the local hunt. The rather ordinary brick residence was superseded by the present mansion that was built on a grand scale in the late 18TH

century for the 3RD Duke by the architect James Wyatt. At the same time and in similarly splendid style, the stables were added in distinct contrast to the original, modest hunting lodge that still stands in the grounds today. Lovingly refurbished by present occupants and family of the current Duke, the Earl and Countess of March who live at Goodwood with their young family, Goodwood House is a fascinating place to visit. Several rooms, including the state apartments and magnificent recreated Egyptian dining room are open to visitors for a limited period each year. The history of this aristocratic family is depicted in the paintings and exquisite furnishings and works of art that adorn the rooms. Paintings date back to the family's Royal origins as descendants of Charles II, and traverse the 18th century with the lively Lennox sisters. The family's horses are portrayed by none other than Stubbs and the views from their London home by Canaletto. Other items on display include a fine collection of Sèvres porcelain collected by Duke number three whilst he was Ambassador to Paris, some gruesome relics from the Napoleonic Wars and more exquisite furniture and tapestries from Paris. Additional exhibitions of fine works of art are also assembled for display in the house from time to time.

Famed around the world for the annual Glorious Goodwood race meeting that was first introduced by the 4th Duke of Richmond in 1814 just 12 years after racing first began here, Goodwood racecourse has entertained wealthy socialites and

Goodwood House

racing fanatics with regular meetings throughout the flat season for nearly 200 years. The 12,000 acre Goodwood estate also plays host to the popular Festival of Speed at its classic motor circuit in July as well as the annual nostalgic Revival Meeting.

Sculpture at Goodwood is a changing collection of specially commissioned contemporary British sculpture set in the beautiful grounds, and there's an aerodrome and a golf course if you're in the mood for some more sporting action.

Sculpture at Goodwood - Host by Peter Burke

HALNAKER
3½ miles NE of Chichester on the A285

Pronounced Hannacker, this village was the seat of the influential and powerful De La Warr family. The present **Halnaker House**, designed by Edwin Lutyens in 1938, is a splendid modern country house. However, just to the north lies the original Halnaker House which was allowed to fall into decay around 1800 - just as the residents of nearby Goodwood House were commanding attention within London's society. Built in medieval times, the old house was originally the home of the De Haye family who were also the founders of Boxgrove Priory.

Above the village, on Halnaker Hill, stands an early 18TH century tower windmill, **Halnaker Windmill**, which remained in use until 1905 when it too was allowed to fall into ruin. In 1912, Hilaire Belloc mentioned the windmill in a poem in which he compares the decay of agriculture in Britain with the neglected mill. The exterior was restored in 1934 and the windmill was used as an observation tower during World War II.

BOXGROVE
2 miles NE of Chichester off the A27

This attractive village is home to the remains of **Boxgrove Priory**, a cell of the Benedictine Lessay Abbey in France which was founded in around 1115. Initially a community of just three monks, over the centuries the priory expanded and grew into one of the most influential in Sussex. However, all that remains today are the Guest House, Chapter House and the Church which is now the parish Church of St Mary and St Blaise. Its sumptuous interior reflects the priory's former importance and, before the Dissolution of the Monasteries, the De La Warr Chantry Chapel was built like a 'church within a church' as the final resting place of the family. Unfortunately, Henry VIII forced De La Warr to dispose of the priory and the family were eventually buried at Broadwater near Worthing. Though it is still empty, the extravagant marble chapel has survived. The Priory also contains a beautiful 16th century ceiling painted by Lambert Barnard and Victorian stained glass.

A fascinating discovery was made, in 1993, by local archaeologists who unearthed prehistoric remains in a local sand and gravel pit. Amongst the finds was an early hominid thigh bone and, whilst there is still some debate over the precise age of the bone, the find has been named **Boxgrove Man.**

TANGMERE
2 miles E of Chichester off the A27

The village is still very much associated with the nearby former Battle of Britain base, RAF Tangmere and, although the runways have now been turned back into farmland or housing estates, the efforts of those brave young men are remembered at the local pub, The Bader Arms (named after pilot Douglas Bader) and **Tangmere Military Aviation Museum.** The museum, based at the airfield, tells the story, through replica aircraft, photographs, pictures, models and memorabilia, of military flying from the earliest days to the present time. The Battle of Britain Hall tells its own story with aircraft remains, personal effects and true accounts from both British and German pilots of those terrifying days in 1940. Many historic aircraft are on display at the airfield including the Hunter and the Meteor which both broke the World Air Speed record in their day actually at the Tangmere airfield. Finally, it was whilst at RAF Tangmere during World War II that EH Bates completed his novel Fair Stood the Wind for France.

SIDLESHAM
4 miles S of Chichester on the B2145

A pleasant village that is home to the **Pagham Harbour Nature Reserve.** The harbour was formed when the sea breached reclaimed land in 1920 and it is now well known for its 200 different species of birds and as a breeding ground for many rare species. The tidal mud flats not only attract an abundance of wildfowl but also many species of animals and

marine life. Sidlesham Ferry is the starting point for guided walks around this important conservation area, which is also one of the few undeveloped stretches of the Sussex Coast.

NORTON
6 miles S of Chichester on the B2145

One of the original communities that made up Selsey (Sutton, the other, is now the present day town), Norton's first church was probably built on, or close to, the site of the cathedral that St Wilfrid erected when he became Bishop of the South Saxons in AD 681. Following the Norman Conquest, the country bishoprics were moved into the towns and Selsey's bishop transferred to Chichester. In the 1860s, the decision to move the medieval parish Church of St Peter from its isolated site to Selsey was taken and it was moved by horse and cart in 1866, and later refurbished and named **St Wilfred's Chapel.**

SELSEY
7 miles S of Chichester on the B2145

Once an important Saxon town, fishing has been the main stay of life here for many centuries. However, according to accounts by the Venerable Bede, St Wilfrid, whilst Bishop of the South Saxons, the Selsey fishermen were so unsuccessful and such was their shortage of food that they were prepared to throw themselves off nearby cliffs. St Wilfrid taught them to fish and the town has thrived ever since. Until recently, only Selsey crabs were served on the QE2.

Now a more modest town yet still a popular resort, the main street still looks much as it did in the 18TH century. The **Sessions House**, where the Lord of Selsey Manor held court, was probably built in the early 17TH century though it still contains the exposed beams and wooden

ST ANDREWS LODGE HOTEL

Chichester Road, Selsey,
West Sussex, PO20 0LX
Tel: 01243 606899 Fax: 01243 607826
e-mail: info@standrewslodge.co.uk
website: www.standrewslodge.co.uk

Situated in the Manhood Peninsula, just outside the historical city of Chichester and on the edge of the town of Selsey, the **St Andrews Lodge Hotel** is set back from the road and has a large secluded garden and ample private parking. All rooms are en-suite and several of its comfortably furnished rooms are located on the ground floor, one of which has been converted for wheelchair access. These rooms look out over the well tended, lawned garden and patio, splashed with colour from overflowing tubs of flowers, at the rear of the house.

Although the Humphreys are not from far away, they have made a dramatic shift in their lifestyle away from the corporate life to run this inviting guest house. The South coast is only one mile away and St Andrews Lodge has golf, fishing, horse riding and seasport facilities nearby for those active moments and a sun trap garden with plenty of chairs and loungers for intensive relaxation. An appetising breakfast is freshly prepared to set you up for the day. St Andrews has a licenced bar serving a selection of bottled beers, lagers, wines, spirits and soft drinks.

panelling of an earlier age. There are also several thatched cottages to be seen, including the 18TH century Cottage and the 16TH century farmhouse known as The Homestead. Perhaps, though, the most impressive building here is **Selsey Windmill**. Today's mill, a tower mill made from local red bricks and the only one of its kind in Sussex, was built in 1820 as the previous late 17TH century timber construction had suffered greatly from weather damage. Though it ceased milling flour in 1910, the mill continued to grind pepper into the 1920s. Now rescued and restored it is a pleasant local landmark, although it can only be admired from the outside.

With so many of the townsfolk dependant upon the sea for their living, the Lifeboat Station was established here in 1860. The present building was erected 100 years later and there is an interesting **Lifeboat Museum**.

For many years the town's **East Beach** was a well recognised scene for smuggling and, in the 18TH century, this was a full time occupation for many local inhabitants. In fact, whilst the French were in the throws of their revolution the villagers of Selsey were busy smuggling ashore over 12,000 gallons of spirits. Much later, during World War II, East Beach was used as a gathering point for sections of the famous Mulberry Harbour that was transported across the Channel as part of the D-Day landings. Just inland from the beach, now on a roundabout, is a small building called the **Listening Post**. During World War I it was used as a naval observation post, with personnel listening out for the sound of invading German airships, and as such it acted as an early warning system long before radar were established.

Geographically, **Selsey Bill**, the extreme southwest of Sussex, is an island with the

English Channel on two sides, Pagham Harbour to the northeast and a brook running from the harbour to Bracklesham Bay which cuts the land off from the remainder of the Manhood Peninsular. However, Ferry Banks, built in 1809, links the bill with the mainland. Over the centuries this part of the coastline has been gradually eroded and many of the area's historic remains have been lost beneath the encroaching tides.

EARNLEY
6 miles SW of Chichester off the B2198

This charming small village is home to **Earnley Gardens**, a delightful place with 17 themed gardens, exotic birds and butterflies and also an unusual museum. **Rejectamenta**, the Museum of 20TH Century Memorabilia, displays thousands of everyday items which reflect the changes in lifestyle over the past 100 years. There is everything here from old washing powder packets and winklepickers to stylophones and space hoppers.

WEST WITTERING
7 miles SW of Chichester on the B2179

West Wittering and its larger neighbour, **East Wittering**, both lie close to the beautiful inlet that is Chichester's natural harbour. A charming seaside village, West Wittering overlooks the narrow entrance to the harbour and this former fishing village has developed into a much sought after residential area and select holiday resort. Here, too, lies **Cakeham Manor House**, with its distinctive early 16TH century brick tower that was once the summer palace of the bishops of Chichester. It was in the manor's studio of this splendid medieval part Tudor and part Georgian house that Sir Henry Royce, of Rolls Royce, designed many of his inventions.

Both villages have easy access to excellent sandy beaches and the headland that forms the eastern approach to Chichester Harbour, East Head, which is now a nature reserve. A sand and shingle spit, one of only six dune systems along the whole of the south coast of England, East Head supports a variety of bird, plant and marine life and also welcomes many migrant wildfowl onto the salt marsh during the winter months.

ITCHENOR
5 miles SW of Chichester off the B2179

In the 13TH century the villagers of Itchenor (originally a Saxon settlement called Icenore) built a church which they

West Wittering Beach

THE SHIP INN

The Street, Itchenor, nr Chichester, West Sussex PO20 7AH
Tel: 01243 512284   Fax: 01243 513817

The aptly named **Ship Inn** is situated close to Chichester Harbour and exactly 6 miles south of the city. Though the current building only dates back to the 1930s, there has been an inn on the site since the early 18th century. This warm and welcoming freehouse is the place to come for excellent food, drink and hospitality. The large bar area and separate restaurant both have a nautical theme. Not surprisingly, given the location, fresh fish and seafood feature heavily on the menu, which is balanced with an equally tempting selection of beef and poultry dishes.

chose to dedicate to St Nicholas, the guardian of seafarers. As the village overlooks the sheltered waters of Chichester Harbour, shipbuilding was an obvious industry to become established here and, as early as the 1600s, there was a shipyard at Itchenor. The last ships built here were minesweepers during World War II but the village today is a busy sailing and yachting centre as well as being the customs clearance port for Chichester Harbour.

BIRDHAM
4 miles SW of Chichester on the A286

The setting for Turner's famous painting of Chichester Harbour (which can be seen at Petworth House), this delightful place is as charming today as it was at the time when the views captured the great artist's imagination. The **Sussex Falconry Centre**, which was originally set up as a breeding and rescue centre for indigenous birds of prey can also be found here. In 1991, the centre started to exhibit the birds to the public and, as well as viewing and watching the birds fly, visitors can also take advantage of the centre's falconry and hawking courses.

FISHBOURNE
2 miles W of Chichester on A286

The village of Fishbourne has its claim to fame in being home to the remains of the largest known Roman residence in Britain, which amazingly were only discovered in 1960 whilst a new water main was being cut. **Fishbourne Roman Palace** was built around AD 75 for the Celtic King Cogidubnus, who collaborated with the Roman conquerors. As well as taking on the role of Viceroy, Cogidubnus was rewarded with this magnificent palace which contained under floor heating, hot baths, a colonnade, an ornamental courtyard garden and lavish decorations. Among the superb remains that can be seen today are a garden and Britain's largest collection of in-situ mosaics, including the famous Boy on a Dolphin.

Fishbourne Roman Palace

The Apple Store

Ridge Farm, Scant Road East, Hambrook, Chichester,
West Sussex, PO18 8UB
Tel: 01243 575567 or 07802 824798 Fax: 01243 576798
e-mail: philip@medlams,co,uk

Aptly named, **The Apple Store** was formerly an apple store,
and is attached to Ridge Farm which occupies a secluded
location set in five acres of scenic pasture land and well
stocked gardens. Its three rooms are tastefully and simply
furnished, and despite being just around the corner from
Goodwood and Fontwell, prices remain static throughout
the year. So it's always a good time to visit!

As well as walking through the excavated remains of the north wing, visitors can see the formal garden which has been replanted to the original Roman plan. When the palace was first constructed the sea came right up to its outer walls and the building remained in use until around AD 320 when a fire largely destroyed the site. The history of the palace, along with many of the artefacts rescued during the excavations, can be discovered in the **Museum**, where there is also an exhibition area on Roman gardening.

BOSHAM
3½ miles W of Chichester off the A286

Pronounced Bozzum, this pleasant village is well known for both its history and its charm. Though it was the Irish monk Dicul who built a small religious house here, Bishop Wilfrid is credited with bringing Christianity to the area in AD 681 and Bosham is probably the first place in Sussex where he preached. Later, in the 10th century, Danish raiders landed here and, amongst the items that they stole, was the church's tenor bell. As the Danes left and took to their boats, the remaining bells were rung to sound the all clear and to indicate to the villagers that they could leave the nearby woods and return to their homes. As the last peal of bells rang out, the tenor bell, in one of the Danish boats, is said to have joined in and, in doing so,

capsized the boat. Both the bell and the sailors sank to the bottom of the creek and the place is now known as **Bell Hole**. Whether the story is true or not nobody knows, but Bosham certainly has its fair share of local legends as the village has strong associations with King Canute. It was here, on the shore, that the king, in the early 11th century, is said to have ordered back the waves in an attempt to

Bosham Harbour

Bosham

demonstrate the limits of his kingly powers. Canute's daughter is buried in the once important Saxon parish church.

Later in the 11TH century, King Harold sailed from Bosham, in 1064, on his ill-fated trip to Normandy to appease his rival, William of Normandy, for the English throne. However, Harold's plans went awry when he was taken captive and made to swear to William to aid his claim to the crown - a promise which, famously, Harold did not keep. It was the breaking of the promise obtained under threat that caused William to set forth with his army a couple of years later. As a result, Harold's lands in Sussex were some of the first to be taken by the conquering army and Bosham church's spire can be seen alongside Harold's ship in the Bayeux Tapestry.

An important port in the Middle Ages

and particularly, between the 1800s and the 20TH century, when it was alive with oyster smacks, Bosham nowadays is a place for keen yachtsmen as well as charming place to explore. The narrow streets that lead down to the harbour are filled with elegant 17TH and 18TH century flint and brick buildings amongst which is the **Bosham Walk Craft Centre**. This fascinating collection of little shops selling all manner of arts, crafts, fashions and antiques within an old courtyard setting, also holds craft demonstrations and exhibitions throughout the summer season.

Bosham House and its beautiful grounds are home to the Bosham Stone – a reputed healing seat and sacred site – as well as to the Hamblin Trust, a registered charity founded in 1960 to continue the work of Henry Thomas Hamblin, known locally as the 'Saint of Sussex' who came to Bosham in 1914 and wrote extensively on a universally spiritual theme. His writing still continues to be distributed throughout the world

WALDERTON
6 miles NW of Chichester off the B2146

Just to the west of the village lies **Stansted House**, a splendid example of late 17TH century architecture. Dating back to the 11TH century when it was a hunting lodge, Stansted has played host to a variety of distinguished guests, including royalty, as well as having several interesting owners over the centuries. The house as it stands today, was built on its present site in 1668 for Richard Lumley - probably by the architect William Talman. Heavily altered in the following two centuries, Stansted House was burnt to the ground in 1900 but, in 1903, the house was rebuilt to the exact plans of Richard Lumley's grand mansion.

Now open to visitors, on a limited basis,

The Barley Mow

Walderton, Near Chichester,
West Sussex, PO18 9EB
Tel: 023 9263 1321

Scarcely visible beneath the mass of creeping ivy and colourful hanging baskets, **The Barley Mow** is a delightful country pub, with its very own wooden floored skittle alley! Although the alley has served many purposes during its lifetime, such as a being a stable, a barn, a bakery and even the base for the local home guard, it is now dedicated to group dining and playing skittles, and a special skittle supper menu including a hot and cold buffet option can be booked in advance.

Owners for most of the past decade, Colin and Lynne Ive have done a great job of decorating the rest of the bar and all its nooks and crannies, using warm wood furniture, dried flowers hanging from the ceiling and old prints, brasses and farm implements adorning the buttermilk yellow walls. Stone floors remain in the original part of the pub, and a large restaurant has been built in a new extension which can accommodate up to 100 diners. Food is standard pub fare such as grills, salads, sandwiches and is supplement by lunchtime specials, vegetarian choices and a lengthy international list of quality wines from both the new and the old world. Outside at the back is a mature lawned beer garden with a barbeque area in which to idle away long, lazy afternoons when the days are hot and sunny.

the house is home to the late Lord Bessborough's collection of paintings and furnishings, including some fine 18TH century tapestries. Meanwhile, the **Below Stairs Experience** transports visitors to the old kitchen, pantry, servants' hall, living quarters and wine cellars, and the surrounding grounds are a haven of peace and tranquility. Finally, the **Stansted Park Garden Centre**, found in the original walled garden and restored Victorian glasshouses of the estate, includes a palm house, camellia house, fernery and vine house.

EAST ASHLING
3 miles NW of Chichester on B2178

A couple of miles to the north of East Ashling lies **Kingley Vale National Nature Reserve**, home probably to the finest yew groves in Europe. A long lived species - 100 years is nothing in the life of a yew tree - the trees were protected until the

mid 16TH century as they were used for making long bows, England's successful weapon against crossbows. Here at Kingley Vale, there are several 500 year old trees although most of the forest is made up of trees approaching their 100TH birthday. Towards the summit of **Bow Hill**, the trees give way to heather and open heathland and here a group of four Bronze Age burial mounds, known as the King's Graves or Devil's Humps, can be found.

ARUNDEL

A settlement since before the Romans invaded, this quiet and peaceful town, which lies beneath the battlements of one of the most impressive castles in the country, was a strategically important site where the major east-west route through Sussex crosses the River Arun. One of

William the Conqueror's most favoured knights, Roger de Montgomery, first built a castle here, on the high ground overlooking the river, in the late 11TH century. With a similar plan to that of Windsor castle, **Arundel Castle** consisted of a motte with a double bailey, a design which, despite rebuilding and several alterations, remains clearly visible today. The second largest castle in England, it has been the seat of the Dukes of Norfolk and the Earls of Arun for over 700 years.

Arundel Castle

Very badly damaged in 1643 when, during the Civil War, Parliamentarian forces bombarded it with canons fired from the church tower, a programme of restoration took place during the late 18TH century to make it habitable once more. A second programme of rebuilding was undertaken 100 years later by the 15TH Duke of Norfolk, using profits from the family's ownership of the newly prosperous steel town of Sheffield. Unfortunately, all that remains today of the original construction are the 12TH century shell keep and parts of the 13TH century barbican and curtain wall.

However, despite the rebuilding work of the 18TH and 19TH century, the castle is still an atmospheric place to visit. The state apartments and main rooms contain some fine furniture dating from the 16TH century and there are some excellent tapestries and paintings by Reynolds, Van Dyck, Gainsborough, Holbein and Constable on show. Of the more personal items to be seen are the possessions of Mary, Queen of Scots and a selection of heraldic artefacts from the Duke of Norfolk's collection. The title, the Duke of

Norfolk, was first conferred on Sir John Howard in 1483, by his friend Richard III, and, as well as carrying the hereditary office of Earl Marshal of England the Duke of Norfolk is also the premier duke of England. The Howard family had several famous members including Lord Howard of Effingham who along with Drake repelled the Armada, and the 3rd Duke of Norfolk who was the uncle of two of Henry VIII's wives Anne Boleyn and Catherine Howard. The ancient tombs of the Norfolk family can be seen in the Fitzalan Chapel.

Perhaps the most gruesome item to be seen at the castle can be found, not surprisingly, in the armoury. The **Morglay Sword**, which measures five feet nine inches long, is believed to have belonged to Bevis, a castle warden who was so tall that it was said he could walk from Southampton to Cowes without getting his head wet. In order to determine his final resting place, Bevis, so the story goes, threw his sword off the castle's battlements and, half a mile away, where the sword landed, is a mound that is still known as Bevis's Grave.

The period of stability that the castle brought to the town in late medieval times

THE COPPER KETTLE

21 Tarrant Street, Arundel, West Sussex, BN18 9DG
Tel: 01903 883679

Sussex born and bred Steve Piggott has every reason to be proud of **The Copper Kettle**, a charming restaurant and tea room located in the middle of the ancient settlement of Arundel, which has been a part of the town's history for around 480 years. Tudor in origin, the building has a projecting upper storey (a jetty) covering a timber frame, and is the only surviving example of its kind in the town. Wood from old sailing ships was used to build the black painted beams which contrast starkly with the white brick walls.

Essentially a tea shop during the day serving light

meals and tempting tea time treats, the Copper Kettle has a soft pastel walls and delicate lace table cloths. In the evening it metamorphosises into a romantic, candle lit restaurant with seating inside and out on the patio. Cuisine is based on modern British favourites and it locally sourced where possible, and freshly prepared by owner Steve Piggott, who has spent 20 years working in the catering industry.

Steve has stamped his own ideas on many of the dishes that he has developed during his career. Diners are efficiently looked after by a team of attentive and courteous staff.

turned Arundel into an important port and market town. In fact, the port of Arundel was mentioned in the Doomsday Book and it continued to operate until the 20TH century when it finally closed in 1927 - the last Harbour Master was moved to Shoreham and the port transferred to Littlehampton.

It was also during this peaceful period that the 14th century parish Church of St Nicholas was built - a unique church in that it is divided into separate Catholic and Anglican areas by a Sussex iron screen. Despite religious persecution, particularly during the 16th century, the Fitzalan family and the successive Dukes of Norfolk remained staunch Catholics. So much so, that the 15th Duke, who was responsible for the 19th century rebuilding of the castle, also commissioned the substantial Catholic Church of St Philip Heri which was designed by JA Hansom and Son, the

inventors of the Hansom cab, in 1870. In 1965, this impressive building became the seat of the Catholic bishopric of Brighton and Arundel and was renamed the **Cathedral of Our Lady and St Philip Howard.** (Sir Philip was the 13th Earl of Arundel who died in prison after being sentenced to death by Elizabeth I for his beliefs.) Each year in June, the cathedral hosts the two day Corpus Christi Festival during which the entire length of the aisle is laid out with a carpet of flowers. carpet of flowers consisting of 30,000 blooms.

Another good time to visit is for the Arundel Festival, centred around the August bank holiday and featuring all sorts of drama, concerts and light hearted entertainment.

Other historic sites in the town include the **Maison Dieu**, a medieval hospital outside one of the castle's lodges, that was founded by Richard Fitzalan in 1345.

ARUNDEL WILDFOWL AND WETLANDS CENTRE

Mill Road, Arundel,
West Sussex BN18 9PB
Tel: 01903 883355 Fax: 01903 884834
e-mail: info.arundel@wwt.org.uk
website: www.wwt.org.uk

Have a fantastic day out seeing, feeding, and learning about wetland birds and wildlife, and at the same time help the Wildfowl & Wetlands Trust to conserve wetland habitats and their biodiversity.

WWT was founded in 1946 by the artist and naturalist Sir Peter Scott and is the largest international wetland conservation charity in the UK. WWT Arundel is one of 9 centres and it consists of more than 60 beautiful acres of ponds, lakes and reed beds. WWT Arundel is home to over 1000 of the world's most spectacular ducks, geese and swans, many of which are rare or endangered. This includes the world's rarest goose, the Nene, which was saved from extinction by WWT. Also see the New Zealand Blue Ducks -

WWT Arundel is also the only site in the world outside of New Zealand where Blue Ducks have successfully bred. You can enjoy an atmospheric stroll through the reed beds on the new boardwalk, or watch wild birds from one of the many hides. Kids can follow the themed Discovery trail through the grounds. WWT Arundel also features the award winning recreation of the volcanic Lake Myvatin, complete with lava formations, waterfalls, and it's native duck the common Scoter which is part of a specialist breeding programme. There is also plenty to do inside the centre - the new Eye of the Wind wildlife art gallery shows a continuous programme of local and national wildlife artists, many of whom host art workshops at the centre. You can enjoy superb homemade food in the Waters Edge Restaurant situated in the main viewing gallery overlooking swan lake, or browse through the gift shop or *In Focus* (telescope and binocular specialists) shop.

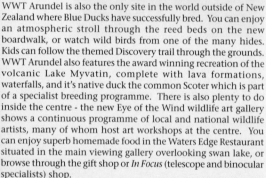

Special events run throughout the year, and there are children's crafts every school holiday. Open every day except Christmas day. Less than 1 mile from Arundel town centre (follow the brown duck signs). Free parking. 20 minute walk from Arundel train station.

WWT Arundel

The most complete year round wildlife experience in Sussex!

Dissolved by Henry VIII 200 years later, this semi monastic institution combined the roles of clinic, hotel and almshouse. For a greater insight into the history of the town and its various inhabitants down the ages, the **Arundel Museum and Heritage Centre** is well worth a visit, and an audio guided tour - the Arundel History Tour - is available from the Arundel visitor centre so you can learn as you stroll around this historic centre.

Blackfriars, the remains of a Dominican Priory located by the bridge over the River Arun is also worth seeking out, and if you're looking for some locally made crafts, to take home, English Country Crafts is the place to head for.

Just to the north of the city, is the **Wildlife and Wetland Trust** (see panel below), part of the largest international wetland conservation charity in the UK and inhabited by ducks, geese and swans from all over the world. There is an award winning visitor centre and a recreation of an Icelandic volcanic lake, a gallery showing exhibitions from leading environmental and wildlife artists and plenty of bird watching hides from which to spy on the residents.

AROUND ARUNDEL

BURPHAM
2 miles NE of Arundel off the A27

This attractive downland village of flint and brick built thatched cottages overlooks the River Arun and provides excellent views of Arundel Castle. The peace and quiet found here seems far removed from the days when the Saxons built defensive earthworks in an attempt to keep the invading Danes at bay. Later, during the Middle Ages, one of the farms on nearby Wepham Down was a leper colony and the track leading down into

the village is still known as Lepers' Way.

LYMINSTER
1½ miles S of Arundel on the A284

Lyminster is an ancient settlement of flint cottages and protective walls which appears, as *Lullyngminster*, in Alfred the Great's will of AD 901. From the village there is a marvellous view of Arundel Castle looking, this time, northwest across the water meadows of the lower River Arun. Local legend has it that the deep pool, known as the **Knuckler Hole**, which lies northwest of Lyminster church, was once inhabited by a savage sea dragon whose only food was fair maidens. This monster was said to have terrorised the local population to such an extent that the King of Wessex offered half his kingdom and his daughter's hand in marriage to the man who killed the beast. The dragon was finally slain after a terrible fight though there is some confusion regarding the identity of the brave dragon slayer, who it is said was either a gallant, young farm boy known as Jim Pulk or a more traditional, handsome knight. Both stories, however, agree that the early Norman coffin slab in the north transept of the church is where the conquering hero was finally laid to rest and it is still known as the **Slayer's Stone**.

LITTLEHAMPTON
3 miles S of Arundel on the A284

This is a charming maritime town, at the mouth of the River Arun, that is also an ancient site - signs of Roman occupation have been discovered here and the local manor is mentioned in the Domesday Book. Following the Norman invasion, Littlehampton became an important Channel port (declining considerably in the 1500s), exporting timber from the Sussex Weald and importing stone from Caen, France. It was here, too, that Queen Matilda arrived from France, in 1139, to stake her unsuccessful claim to the English throne from Stephen.

Now a quiet and pleasant coastal town and a popular holiday resort, though not as fashionable as many of its larger neighbours, Littlehampton does have all the ingredients for a traditional seaside break - a large amusement complex, a boating marina, a lively promenade and a harbour, where **Littlehampton Fort** can also be found. Built in 1764 in the shape of a crescent it is now hidden by vegetation. However, the town's most charming feature is, undoubtedly, the large green which lies between the seafront and the first row of houses.

The easily accessible, gently sloping sand of the East Beach provides safe and foot friendly bathing in contrast to the wild and untamed dunes across the Arun estuary on the West Beach. For a spot of boat watching, the lifeboat station or Littlehampton Harbour with its commercial and fishing boat occupants are

the places to go. Alternatively, plan your visit during August to coincide with the spectacular Littlehampton Regatta.

A visit to **Littlehampton Museum,** extensively refurbished thanks to the Heritage Lottery Fund, reveals the town's maritime history as well as the story of the area displaying objects used by local people over the past 500 years. Still on a maritime theme, the town centre also has a distinctly nautical flavour and hosts a weekly market on Fridays and Saturdays.

FELPHAM
5 miles SW of Arundel off the A259

Alfred the Great ruled the roost here in the 9th century, and the village's other claim to fame is that poet and artist, William Blake, moved here, along with his wife and sister, in 1800 in order to undertake some engraving work for William Hayley, a gentleman of the period. The cottage where the Blakes lived can still be seen

THE BLACK HORSE INN

Climping Street, Climping,
West Sussex, BN17 5RL
Tel: 01903 715175 Fax: 01903 732556
website: www.blackhorseclimping.co.uk

In its former role as a coaching inn some 400 years ago, **The Black Horse Inn** close to the famous Climping Beach was a frequent haunt of smugglers. Nowadays the clientele tends to be less sinister in this typical country Inn, which also houses three en-suite rooms, thoughtfully furnished with plenty of creature comforts. Whitewashed walls are dotted with vibrant hanging baskets and behind the pretty lace curtains that hang at the small, cottage style windows the interior is adorned with dried flowers, brasses, copper kettles and jugs and an assortment of other curios.

Open plan seating in the bar is complemented by snug little nooks and crannies in which to while away the hours enjoying a meal with your friends and family. As the Inn becomes ever more popular it is recommended to call in advance to book your table and avoid any disappointment. The kitchen can handle an impressive 200 covers, serving everything from freshly cut sandwiches to daily fresh fish, hearty gammons, and a wide choice of generous steaks along with a daily specials board. The chefs do all possible to source fresh local produce along with fresh herbs grown in the Inn's own kitchen garden. Owners Chris Connor and Simon Bibby with their team delight in extending a warm welcome to all who visit, be it their first or one of many.

down Blake's Road and it was whilst here that he wrote 'Away to sweet Felpham for Heaven is there' which recalls the view of the sea from his window as well as the words to that most nationalistic of hymns, Jerusalem and the preface to Milton. He left the village a few years later after being tried and acquitted of sedition in Chichester.

Bognor Regis

BOGNOR REGIS
6 miles SW of Arundel on the A259

One very good reason for visiting Bognor Regis is that it holds the title of being the sunshine capital of Britain. Selsey Bill and the Isle of Wight plus the effect of the South Downs shelter it from any passing clouds, so for the past decade it has basked in more sunshine than anywhere else in the British Isles.

Towards the end of the 18th century, before this sunny town became the popular resort that it is today, Sir Richard Hotham, a wealthy London milliner and MP noted the healthy climate in, what was then, a sleepy village on the Sussex coast, and went about trying to transform Bognor into a into a fashionable resort to rival Brighton. He set about constructing some imposing residences, including The Dome in Upper Bognor Road, and even planned to have the town renamed Hothampton. Unfortunately, the fashionable set of the day stayed away and Hotham's dream was never realised - at least not in his lifetime. However, in 1929, George V came to the resort to convalesce following a serious illness and, on the strength of his stay, the town was granted the title Regis (meaning of the King). Today, the town is a pleasant coastal resort

with some elegant Georgian features, traditional public gardens, a promenade and safe, sandy beaches.

Hotham Park House and Gardens, built by the man himself in 1792 are key features on the Bognor map. Visitors can enjoy concerts here given at the bandstand, clock golf, tennis and strolling around the naturally planted areas. The **Bognor Regis Museum**, housed in a lodge of Hotham Park, plays tribute to Sir Richard Hotham as well as telling the story of the famous bathing machine lady, Mary Wheatland, and the important stay of George V. Mary Wheatland was a well known Bognor Regis character: born in 1835 in the nearby village of Aldinbourne she would hire out bathing machines as well as teach children to swim and she also saved many souls from drowning for which she received medals and recognition from the Royal Humane Society. The sea air and exercise must have done the eccentric lady a great deal of good as she lived to be 89 years old.

And perhaps it was the healthy climate that attracted the succession of royal children who have holidayed in Bognor. Bognor's other royal connection is the drinking fountain that commemorates Queen Victoria's Diamond Jubilee set amongst the many fine listed buildings on **The Steyne** built between 1820 and 1840, where author Lewis Carrol once stayed at no 6.

Another museum worthy of a mention is the Bognor Regis **Wireless Museum**, which provides a fascinating trip down memory lane to the time of crystal receivers, and you can even try your hand at morse code. Arts and crafts fans should take a look in the **Rose Green Art & Craft Centre** to catch up with the local art scene or to view a demonstration by a craftsman.

But Bognor is perhaps best known for its "Birdmen" and the annual international Birdman Rally held in August. The competitors, in a variety of classes, take it in turns to hurl themselves off the pier in a jaw-dropping collection of modified hanggliders and aeronautical inventions in an attempt to make the longest unpowered flight and so win the coveted competition - definitely a sight worth seeing!

YAPTON
3½ miles SW of Arundel on the B2233

Set amid the wheat fields of the coastal plain, this village has a charming 12TH century church, the tower of which leans at an alarming angle.

FONTWELL
3½ miles W of Arundel off the A27

The village is well known to followers of horse racing as it is home to the pleasantly situated **Fontwell Park National Hunt Racecourse**. First opened in 1921, the unusual 'figure of eight' track holds 15 meetings between August and May and remains a firm favourite with jumping enthusiasts. Fontwell is also the home of **Denman's Garden**, a beautifully sheltered, 3.5 acre semi-wild, 20TH century garden once part of the estate owned by Lord Denman in the 19th century. A large Dutch light greenhouse contains unusual frost tender species, and outside the emphasis in planting is on colour, shape and texture which can be appreciated all year round.

SLINDON
3 miles NW of Arundel off the A29

With a dramatic setting on the side of a slope of the South Downs, this pretty village has been occupied as an excellent observation point right from Neolithic times, and many fine examples of early flint tools have been found in the area. The name itself is derived from the Saxon word for sloping hill.

The picturesque village of Slindon stands on a shelf of the South Downs and was the estate village for Slindon House. Today, the **Slindon Estate**, the largest National Trust owned estate in Sussex, which includes most of the village, the woodlands and Slindon House (now let to Slindon College) offers plenty to see as well as excellent opportunities for walking and birdwatching. Slindon House was originally founded as a residence for the Archbishops of Canterbury. (Archbishop Stephen Langton, a negotiator and signatory of the Magna Carta, spent the last weeks of his life here in 1228.) Rebuilt in the 1560s and extensively remodelled during the 1920s, the house is now a private boys' school. The estate's wonderful post office is an amalgamation of two 400 year old cottages and it is the village's only remaining thatched building. The focal point of the village is the crossroads where a tree stands in a small open area close to the village church. Dating from the 12TH century, this charming flint built church contains an unusual reclining effigy of a Tudor knight, Sir Anthony St Leger, the only wooden carving of its kind in Sussex. Finally, just to the north lies the cricket field where Sir Richard Newland is said to have refined the modern game over 200 years ago.

From the village there is a splendid walk around the estate that takes in the ancient deer park of Slindon House as well as other remains such as the summerhouse. The magnificent beech trees found in the woodland were once highly prized and their seeds were sold worldwide. Unfortunately, the severe storm of October 1987 flattened many of these beautiful trees, some of which had stood for 250 years. Though most were cleared, some were left and the dead wood has provided new habitats for a whole range of insects and fungi. Birds and other wild life also abound in the woodlands and, in May, the floor becomes covered with a carpet of bluebells.

WORTHING

Despite having been inhabited since the Stone Age, Worthing remained a small and isolated fishing community until the end of the 18th century when the popularity of sea bathing among the rich and fashionable set led to a period of rapid development. The climax to this period of development occurred in 1798, when George III sent his 16 year old daughter, Princess Amelia, to Worthing to recuperate from an ill-fated affair with one of his royal equerries. By 1830, however, Worthing's Golden Age was at an end but fortunately many of the Georgian town houses, villas and streets can still be seen today, just as they were nearly 200 years ago. Further development work was hampered by the cholera and typhoid outbreaks of the 1850s and 1890s although, between the two World Wars, some more modest expansion was undertaken.

Throughout much of the 19th century, Worthing remained a popular resort with

Trenchers Restaurant & Brasserie

118-120 Portland Road, Worthing, Sussex BN11 1QA
Tel: 01903 820287 Fax: 01903 820305
e-mail: info@trenchersrestaurant.com
website: www.trenchersrestaurant.com

Trenchers is a sophisticated and stylish eatery, which is well known and highly regarded by residents in the surrounding area. Its colourful exterior is reflected on the inside, by modern ,colourful and classy décor which sets the tone for some memorable dining. Run by business partners James Thompson who takes care of front of house and Steve Land who looks after the cooking, with over ten years experience in the trade, Trenchers is deservedly very popular and it's best to book at weekends.

In the 26 seater restaurant an innovative, contemporary a la carte menu draws on international influences with starters like seared scallops on crispy Chinese cabbage with a soy, sesame and ginger dressing and main dishes like Thai roasted duck breast with glass noodle and coriander roll and wok fried greens. Dishes in the 32 seater brasserie such as poached haddock on champ mash with grain mustard sabayon are equally eclectic and tempting. An excellent value wine list combines approachable and easy drinking wines from both new and old world, most of which are also available by the glass, which can also be enjoyed as a pre or post dinner drink in the cosy bar area.

THE RICHARD COBDEN

2 Cobden Road, Worthing, West Sussex BN11 4BD
Tel: 01903 236856
e-mail: rcobdenpub@ntlworld.com
website: www.downourlocal.com/richard-cobden

Sitting on a residential street corner just a short walk from the centre of Worthing, **The Richard Cobden** was built in 1868 and is now a homely and friendly public house. Smartly decorated with typical pub trappings, the pub was named after a well known 19th century member of Parliament. Food is only available at lunchtime, and roasts are particularly popular. On Thursday nights musicians gather here to jam, and customers are welcome to join in.

THISTHAT THEOTHER

Chapel Road, Worthing, West Sussex BN11 1BY
Tel: 01903 238504
e-mail: ni@dysfunktional.co.uk
website: www.dysfunktional.co.uk

With its genuinely fresh, friendly and relaxed approach, **Thisthat** and **Theother** is one of the top destinations in downtown Worthing, bringing an original style and an unparalleled vibe to the town's entertainment scene. Theother is a bar and restaurant open for food and drinks

during the day and in the evening, while Thistat is a nightclub open until 2am, and featuring special music nights and djs.

POPPYFIELD

53 Rowlands Road, Worthing, West Sussex BN11 3JN
Tel: 07905 212579

A joint venture by enthusiastic business partners Mo and Nic, **Poppyfield** is a bright and contemporary café located not far from the town centre and the sea front. Vibrant green and red décor conveys the poppy theme and gives the place a lively feel. Melt in your mouth food ranges from tasty snacks to full blown roast dinners or giant filled Yorkshire puds, and don't worry if you fancy something that's not on the menu, because if they have the ingredients they'll cook it for you!

BLAIR HOUSE HOTEL

11 St Georges Road, Worthing, West Sussex, BN11 2DS
Tel & Fax: 01903 234071
e-mail: stay@blairhousehotel.co.uk
website: www.blairhousehold.co.uk

A short walk from the centre of Worthing and the seafront, the **Blair House Hotel** is one of the best small hotels in the town. Housed in a smart, Victorian house on a residential street, the hotel has seven ensuite rooms. Guests can choose between staying on a B&B basis or booking a traditional English dinner in the licensed dining room.

both royalty and the famous: it was here, in the summer of 1894, that Oscar Wilde wrote *The Importance of Being Ernest* and immortalised the town's name in that of the central character, Jack Worthing. Worthing's **Pier**, one of the country's oldest, was built in the 1860s at the time when a pier was a must for any successful Victorian seaside resort. An elegant construction with a 1930s pavilion at the end, it has, during its lifetime, been blown down, burnt down and blown up! Of the more recent buildings to be found here, the **English Martyrs Catholic Church**, just west of the town centre, is a recommended stopping point. Painted on the ceiling is a replica of Michelangelo's Sistine Chapel fresco that was completed by a local artist in 1993.

As Worthing expanded it also swallowed up a number of ancient nearby settlements including Broadwater with its fine cottages and Norman church and West Tarring where the remains of a 13TH century palace belonging to the Archbishops of Canterbury now double as the village hall and primary school annexe.

Today, Worthing is a bustling seaside town, with all the usual amenities necessary for a true English holiday as well as excellent shopping, dining and entertainment facilities.

For an insight into the history of the town a visit to the **Worthing Museum** and **Art Gallery** is essential. Through a series of fascinating displays, tales of smuggling, the town riots of the 19TH century, top secret activities during World War II and the early life of this fishing village are told. The museum is also home to a nationally important costume and toy collection, and in the surrounding grounds there is a sculpture garden.

Garden lovers are spoilt for choice in Worthing with several town centre gardens to admire and enjoy throughout the year including Denton Gardens, Marine Gardens and the most prestigious, **Beach House Park** which also plays host to the National Bowls Championships, which are held annually in August. **Highdown Chalk Gardens** are also very impressive with an impressive collection of plants from all over the world and pleasant views over the sea and the Downs.

AROUND WORTHING

HIGH SALVINGTON
1½ miles N of Worthing on the A24

This village, now almost entirely engulfed by Worthing, is home to the last survivor of several windmills that once stood in the area. **High Salvington Windmill**, a black post mill, was built between 1700 and

---

The Lamb Inn

Salvington Road, Durrington, Worthing, West Sussex BN13 2JN
Tel: 01903 263356

Husband and wife team Alec and Mary Russell welcome a broad based clientele to **The Lamb Inn**. Set just outside the centre of Worthing, this handsome and imposing pub makes an ideal base for exploring the town. A big, bright lounge provides a spacious and comfortable place to relax and admire the views over the well manicured gardens and outside dining area. Food is a well balanced combination of quality and excellent value for money, with dishes consisting of straightforward pub classics served in very substantial portions.

1720 and its design is one that had been used since the Middle Ages - a heavy cross shaped base with a strong central upright (or post) around which the sails and timber superstructure could pivot. The mill stopped working in 1897 but, following extensive restoration in the 1970s, it has now been restored to full working order and visitors can not only enjoy seeing this magnificent building as it was but also take afternoon tea and marvel at the glorious views.

FINDON
3 miles N of Worthing off the A24

Findon is an attractive village, with a main square surrounded by some elegant 18th century houses and a heavily restored 13TH century village church which now lies on the opposite side of the main road. Situated within the South Downs Area of Outstanding Natural Beauty, Findon is famous for being the venue of one of the two great Sussex sheep fairs - the other is at Lewes. Dating back to the days of the 13TH century when the first markets were held here on Nepcote Green, the annual sheep fair takes place in September and, as well as giving the village a festival atmosphere, over 20,000 sheep change hands here.

From Findon there is also easy access to **Cissbury Ring** strategically perched high up on the Downs looking out over Worthing and the coast. The second

largest Iron Age hill-fort in the country, this impressive overshadowed only by Dorset's Maiden Castle, this impressive hilltop site covers an area of 65 acres and is surrounded by a double rampart almost a mile in circumference. Archaeologists have estimated that over 50,000 tons of chalk, soil and boulders would have had to be moved in the fort's construction which would indicate that this was once a sizeable community in the 3RD century BC. However, the site is much older than this as Neolithic flint mines have also been discovered here that date back 6000 years which also makes Cissbury one of the oldest industrial sites in the country. Today, the site is owned by the National Trust and is open to the public.

COOMBES
4 miles NE of Worthing off the A27

This tiny settlement of just a few houses and a single farm is worthy of a visit if just to see the village church, which stands in the farmyard. An unassuming Norman church it contains some exceptional 12TH century murals that were only uncovered in 1949 and are believed to have been painted by monks from St Pancras Priory, Lewes. Just to the north of the hamlet lies **Annington Hill** from where there are glorious views over the Adur valley and access to a section of the South Downs Way footpath.

FINDON MANOR HOTEL

High Street, Findon, West Sussex, BN14 0TA
Tel: 01903 872733 Fax: 01903 877473

Right at the heart of the picturesque village of Findon, **Findon Manor Hotel** sits amid beautifully designed, mature gardens complete with tropical palm trees. Outside a rambling group of fine, historic buildings started in 1584 gives way to a lavish, country house style interior which highlights the buildings' original features, but combines them with 21st century mod cons.

Rooms are decorated with stylish antiques, including the elegant, calm dining room and lounge which serve traditional Enlgish food, in contrast to the more lively atmosphere at the Snooty Fox bar adjoining the hotel. Conveniently situated as a base for visiting either Worthing, Chichester or Brighton.

SHOREHAM-BY-SEA
4½ miles E of Worthing on the A259

There has been a harbour here, on the River Adur estuary, since Roman times and, though evidence of both Roman and Saxon occupations have been found, it was not until the Norman period that the town developed into an important port. At that time the River Adur was navigable as far as Bramber and the main port was situated a mile or so upstream, where the Norman church of St Nicholas still stands.

However, towards the end of the 11th century, the river estuary began to silt up and the old port and toll bridge were abandoned in favour of New Shoreham, which was built at the river mouth. Again, the Normans built a church, St Mary de Haura, close to the harbour which is today considered one of the greater non-cathedral parish churches, and both churches remain key features of the town.

The old town lapsed into the life of a quiet village whilst, during the 12th and 13th centuries, New Shoreham became one of the most important Channel ports. It was here, in 1199, that King John landed with an army to succeed to the throne of England following the death of Richard the Lionheart and, in 1346, Shoreham was asked to raise 26 ships, more than both Dover and Bristol, to fight the French. Perhaps, though, the town's most historic moment came in 1651 when Charles II fled from here to France, following defeat at the Battle of Worcester, on board the ship of Captain Nicholas Tettersell.

The new port flourished until the 16TH century when, once again, silting, in the form of a shingle spit which diverted the river's course, had disastrous economic consequences. The next 200 years or so saw a period of decline in Shoreham which was only relieved by the rise in

THE CROWN & ANCHOR

33 High Street, Shoreham-by-Sea,
West Sussex, BN43 5DD
Tel: 01273 461753
website: www.crownandanchor.uk.com

A vibrant and unusual pub, the **Crown & Anchor** stands right on Shoreham High Street and overlooks the River Adur at the rear. Its front is dominated by the eyecatching carved figure head and boat jutting out at first floor level. Built in 1745, the Crown & Anchor was built on the site of a pub called the Dolphin, and has been transformed by current leaseholders, Nigel and Lisa Hillyar.

Inside, its creative and vibrantly

colourful 65 seat Riverside Restaurant has high ceilings from which hang marquee style drapes, boarded floors and a huge floor to ceiling window overlooking the rear patio, which is ideally situated for some relaxing al fresco summer drinking with its tranquil views over the river. Food is traditional English, and the extensive choice in the menu is supplemented by an ever changing specials board. Choose from light snacks like jacket potatoes or more substantial dishes like steaks, plus look out for the excellent fresh fish dishes. Entertainment also features strongly at the Crown & Anchor, with a weekly karaoke night and live music on Saturday nights.

THE ROYAL COACH

Brighton Road, Shoreham-By-Sea, West Sussex, BN43 5LD
Tel: 01273 454077 e-mail: graham@theroyalcoach.co.uk
Fax: 01273 440013 website: www.theroyalcoach.co.uk

A large and popular public house and restaurant , the **Royal Coach** is set just back from the seafront at Shoreham. Current leaseholders, Graham and Sara Eaves have firmly stamped their personalities on the establishment by creating a fun weekly program me of entertainment including a weekly quiz night and an in-house pool competition. Real ale fans should plan a visit during the beer festival, when 12 ales are available for tasting, and extensive variety of food options such as light bites, salads, fresh fish, typical pub grub and tempting table d'hote menus can be consumed in the bar or 100 seat restaurant.

popularity of nearby Brighton and the excavation of a new river course in 1818. To reflect its new importance, **Shoreham Fort** was constructed at the eastern end of the beach as part of Palmerston's coastal defence system. A half-moon shape, the fort was capable of accommodating six guns which could each fire 80 pounds of shot. The remains of this Napoleonic fort have been restored and is now open to visitors who will also have a superb view of the still busy harbour. If you're in search of further panoramic views, take a jaunt up Mill Hill, famous for its butterflies, and look out over the Adur Valley

The history of Shoreham-by-Sea and, in particular, its maritime past, are explored at **Marlipins Museum**. The museum is itself interesting, as it is housed in one of the oldest surviving non religious buildings in the country. A Norman customs warehouse, the building was given, in the 14TH century, an unusual knapped flint and Caen stone chequerwork façade. It also has a single 42 foot beam supporting the first floor.

Though the town's past is undoubtedly built upon its port, **Shoreham Airport**, opened in 1936, is the country's oldest commercial airport. Still a major base for recreational flying, the lovely art deco terminal acts as a departure and arrivals hall for many business passengers travelling to and from the Channel Islands and Western Europe. Also here, housed in

a World War II blister hangar, is the **Museum of D-Day Aviation**. With a unique air sea rescue gallery and a collection of early aircraft including a Spitfire and artefacts, uniforms and medals from the desperate days of 1940, the museum is open during the week in the summer season. Tours of the airport can also be booked.

NORTH LANCING
3 miles E of Worthing off the A27

This attractive downland village, with its curved streets, has one of the most ancient Saxon names in Sussex. It is derived from Wlencing, one of the sons of Aella, who led the first Saxon invasion to the area in AD 477. Apart from the old flint cottages on the High Street, the old 13TH century church adds to the timeless atmosphere of the village. However, North Lancing is dominated by a much more recent addition to its skyline - Lancing College. Set high up on a beautiful site overlooking the River Adur, the college was founded in 1848 by Nathaniel Woodward, whose aim was to establish a group of classless schools. By the time of his death in 1891, there were 15 schools in the Woodward Federation and, today, Lancing College is an independent secondary school. Of the college buildings, the splendid 19TH century Gothic style **Chapel** is the most striking and is considered to be one of the finest examples of its kind.

THE SMUGGLERS RESTAURANT

West Street, Sompting, West Sussex BN15 0AP
Tel: 01903 236072 e-mail: peterbench@smugglers17.freeserve.co.uk
Fax: 01903 234886 website: www.smugglers-at-sompting.co.uk

Set in the quaint, little hamlet of Sompting famous for its historic Saxon church with its fine Rhenish Helm spire tower, and just east of the bustling resort of Worthing, **The Smugglers Restaurant** is extremely popular with a mixture of more mature and corporate customers. Family run for many years by Peter and Jan Bench with the help of their son Ricky who tends to pitch in and do a bit of everything, the Smugglers has established a well deserved reputation for serving excellent sea fresh fish and fine local beef in its nautically themed restaurant.

SOMPTING
2 miles E of Worthing off the A27

This village, the name of which means marshy ground, has as its pride and joy, a church that is unique in Britain. Built on foundations which can be traced back to AD 960, the **Church of St Mary** has a distinctive spire that consists of four diamond shaped faces which taper to a point. Known as a Rhenish helm, the design was popular in German Rhineland but is not found elsewhere in this country. In 1154, the church was given to the Knights Templar who completely rebuilt it except for the spire which they left untouched. Just over 150 years later the building came into the hands of their rivals, the Knights Hospitallers, who were responsible for the present design of the church as they returned it to its original Saxon style.

THE HENTY ARMS

2 Ferring Lane, Ferring,
West Sussex BN12 6QY
Tel: 01903 241254 Fax: 01903 503796

Built in 1830 for estate workers, the pub was extended in the 1920s and re-named **The Henty Arms** after the local lord of the manor. Set in the village of Ferring next to the railway line, the pub has a smart red brick and cream front with emerald green window frames on the ground floor bay windows and European style shutters on the first floor . Inside, the

décor is classic and minimalist, with elegant furnishings and snug real fires.

A fine selection of beers, stouts and ales includes Flowers Original and Youngs Special as well as a rotating guest ale. Cooking is fresh and delicious, and is served at lunchtimes and in the evenings eithe r in the main pub or in the separate, airy 26 seater restaurant with its smart, white clothed tables and long picture windows. There's also a large rear garden and a small one out front, which are visited by Morris dancers in August. Current tenants Vernon and Carol Carlyle extend a warm and friendly welcome to regulars and visiting guests throughout the year.

GORING-BY-SEA
1½ miles W of Worthing on the A259

Until the arrival of the railway in the mid 19TH century, this was a small fishing village. However, the Victorians love of a day by the seaside saw the rapid growth of Goring and today it is a genteel place with a pleasant suburban air.

To the northwest stands the cone-shaped **Highdown Hill**, which, although only 266 feet high, stands out above the surrounding coastal plain rewarding energetic climbers on a clear day with views of the Isle of Wight, Selsey Bill, Chichester Cathedral, Arundel Castle, Brighton and Beachy Head. Its prominent nature has led it to be a much sought after vantage point and it is now an important archaeological site owned by the National Trust and containing a late Bronze Age settlement and an early Iron Age hill fort with a pagan Saxon cemetery within the ramparts. The exceptional white painted country house, on the northern side of the hill, is **Castle Goring** and it was built in this elaborate Italian style for the grandfather of the poet Percy Bysshe Shelley.

Close by is **Highdown Gardens**, the creation of Sir Frederick and Lady Stern, who spent over 50 years turning what was originally a chalk pit into a stunning garden. One of the least known gardens in the area, Highdown has a unique collection of rare plants and trees which the couple brought back from their expeditions to the Himalayas and China in the mid 20TH century. The garden was left to the local borough council on the death of Sir Frederick in 1967 and has since been declared a national collection.

2 The West Sussex Downs

The southern boundary to this part of West Sussex is the South Downs, a magnificent range of rolling chalk hills grazed by sheep and cattle that extend for over 50 miles.

Petworth House and Gardens

The South Downs Way, a long distance bridleway follows the crest of the hills from Winchester to Beachy Head at Eastbourne and, whether taken as a whole or enjoyed in sections, it provides splendid views of this Area of Outstanding Natural Beauty as well as a wealth of delightful rural hamlets and villages to discover.

To the north of the Downs lies Midhurst, the home of the area's most famous ruin - Cowdray Park. Though the once splendid Tudor mansion has been reduced to a burnt out shell following a fire in the late 18TH century, the ruins provide a haunting backdrop to the parkland's famous polo matches. Fortunately, there are other grand country houses in this western part of the county that have withstood the ravages of time. In particular, there is Uppark, where HG Wells spent many hours in the great library as a boy and Petworth House, an elegant late 17TH century building that is reminiscent of a French château.

Bignor Roman Villa

Other great names from the world of the arts have also found this region inspirational, the novelist Anthony Trollope spent his last years at South Harting, the poet Tennyson lived under the wooded slopes of Black Down and the composer Edward Elgar visited Fittleworth several times and wrote his famous cello concerto whilst staying there in 1917.

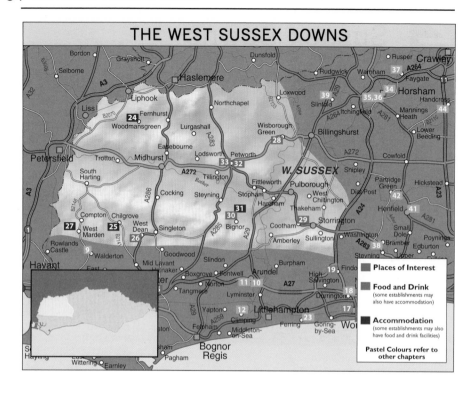

PLACES TO STAY, EAT, DRINK AND SHOP

Midhurst

MIDHURST

Though this quiet and prosperous market town has its origins in the early Middle Ages, its name is Saxon and suggests that once it was surrounded by forest. It was the Norman lord, Savaric Fitzcane, who first built a fortified house here, on the summit of St Ann's Hill, and, though only a few stones remain today, the views from this natural vantage point over the River Rother are worth the walk.

The town of Midhurst grew up at the castle gates and by 1300, when the de Bohuns (the then lords of the manor) moved from their hilltop position the town was well established. Choosing a new site by the river in a coudrier, or hazel grove, provided the family with the name for their new estate - Cowdray. In the 1490s, the estate passed by marriage to Sir David Owen, the natural son of Owen Glendower, and from then on until his death in 1535, Sir David built the splendid Tudor courtyard mansion. However, due to rising debts he was forced to sell the house to Sir William Fitzwilliam, a leading figure in the court of

Henry VIII and the 1st Earl of Southampton. The finishing touches were added by him and his family and, when complete, the magnificent house became a great rival to Hampton Court. Indeed, the house played host to many notable visitors including both Henry VIII and Elizabeth I who were frequently entertained here. Even though the house is now in ruins following a devastating fire in 1793, it is still a splendid monument to courtly Tudor architecture. Today, visitors can view the roofless remains of the east side of the quadrangle court, along with parts of the west side where the turreted three storey gatehouse still remains largely intact. However, most visitors come to **Cowdray Park** to watch the polo matches that take place every weekend from April until July, and in particular the Cowdray Gold Cup.

Back in the town, on the opposite side of the River Rother from Cowdray Park, there are some other impressive buildings including the 16th century timber framed **Market Hall** which is now the home of the famous Midhurst Grammar School that was founded in 1672. **The Spread Eagle Inn**, an old coaching inn, is

Cowdray Park

however older and dates from the 1400s. Though the centre of the town has migrated away from its old heart around the market square and the church, the custom of ringing the curfew each night at 20.00 from the heavily restored church continues and is said to be in memory of a legendary commercial traveller. Whilst endeavouring to reach Midhurst, the traveller got lost in the local woods at dusk and, on hearing the sound of the church bells, was able to find his way safely to the town.

For most people visiting Midhurst, it is through the books of HG Wells that they feel that they already know the town. Wells' maternal grandmother came from Midhurst and his mother worked at nearby Uppark where, as a young boy, Wells spent many hours in the library. At the age of 15, Herbert George was apprenticed to a chemist in the town and also enrolled at the Grammar School for evening classes.

Though he left Midhurst for some years, Wells later returned to the Grammar School as a teacher lodging above a sweet shop in North Street. As well as providing the inspiration for his most famous book *The Invisible Man*, Midhurst has been the setting for many of his short stories including *The Man Who Could Work Miracles*. The great novelist and science fiction writer obviously had fond recollections of his time in the town for he wrote in his autobiography: 'Midhurst has always been a happy place for me. I suppose it rained there at times, but all my memories of Midhurst are in sunshine.' Look out for the blue commemorative plaques to trace Well's movements around the town.

A couple of miles west of Midhurst is the **Iping and Stedham Common Nature Reserve**. This area of lowland heath supports a wide variety of wildlife and grazing Shetland cattle.

WOODMANS GREEN FARM

Linch, West Sussex, GU30 7NF
Tel: 01428 741250
e-mail: peterandmary@woodmansgreen.fsnet.co.uk

Personable hosts, Mary and Peter Spreckley have created a cosy and comfortable environment in which to relax at **Woodmans Green** Farm, deep in the heart of the tranquil Sussex countryside, just 3½ miles from Midhurst. Set in peaceful gardens on a working farm with its own herd of suckler cattle, plus a few chickens, two cats and Max the retriever, this beautiful 16th century farmhouse is full of character with its old stone, tile hung exterior, French doors leading from the lounge to the garden, an open fire in the dining room and exposed beams throughout. Bedrooms are prettily furnished using floral patterns in a country cottage style.

On hot summer days, there's an outdoor swimming pool heated to a toasty warm 75C, and plenty of woods and fields surrounding the garden to explore. The South coast near the artistic centre of Chichester is only a short drive away, and walkers can choose from the endless rolling South Downs or the Sussex Border Path which runs to the north. A hearty English breakfast is cooked by the Spreckleys, and evening meals using much home grown produce can be prepared by prior arrangement. Not surprisingly this is a popular retreat and guests tend to keep on coming back for more!

AROUND MIDHURST

EASEBOURNE
1 mile N of Midhurst on the A272

This delightful estate village, which has some superb half timbered houses, was the home of an Augustinian convent of the Blessed Virgin Mary. Founded in the 13th century, the convent prospered until 1478, when the prioress and some of her nuns were accused of gross immorality and squandering the convent's funds on hunting and extravagant entertaining. All that remains today of the priory is the much restored parish church that was the priory church. Inside is Lord Montague's funeral monument, a fabulous piece of late Tudor sculpture. Another interesting building here is **Budgenor Lodge** which, when it was built in 1793, was a model workhouse and as such was much admired by visiting dignitaries.

FERNHURST
4½ miles N of Midhurst on the A286

Just to the east of this pretty village, with its assorted tile hung cottages surrounding the village green, lies **Black Down**, rising abruptly from the Sussex Weald. A sandstone hill covered in gorse and silver birch, which is particularly spectacular in summer when the heather is in bloom. It is an ideal environment for a variety of upland birdlife, the summit is the highest point in Sussex and from here there are views over the Weald and South Downs to the English Channel.

A particularly fine viewpoint, known as the **Temple of the Winds**, lies on the southern crest and one of the footpaths up the hill has been named locally as **Tennyson's Lane**, after the famous poet who, inspired by the landscape, built his house here and lived in the area for 20 years. At one time a Royal navy signal

tower stood on Tally Knob, a prominent outcrop to the southeast of the Temple of the Winds. In 1796 as a development of the tried and tested system of fire beacons, the Admiralty introduced the Shutter Telegraph here as a more sophisticated means of passing messages between Portsmouth and London. Though ingenious, the system was found to be impractical and was soon abandoned.

To the west of Fernhurst, in the late 12TH century, an Augustinian priory, on an altogether less grand scale then the magnificent Michelham Priory which lies near Upper Dicker, was founded. At the time of the Dissolution the priory became a farmhouse and one of the first floor rooms, which was originally the prior's chamber, is decorated with Tudor murals.

LURGASHALL
4½ miles NE of Midhurst off the A283

This delightful rural village has, as a backdrop, the wooded slopes of Black Down, where Tennyson lived at **Aldworth House**. The village's largely Saxon church has an unusual loggia, or porch, outside where those who had travelled from afar could eat and rest before or after the service.

LODSWORTH
2½ miles E of Midhurst off the A272

Situated on the River Lod, a small tributary of the River Rother, this old community has some fine buildings including a 13TH century manor house and an early 18TH century Dower House. The whitewashed village Church of St Peter lies on the outskirts of Lodsworth and, just to the north is **St Peter's Well**, the water of which is supposed to have healing qualities.

TILLINGTON
5 miles E of Midhurst on the A272

Dating back to the days before the

Norman Conquest - the village appeared in the Domesday Book as Tolinstone - Tillington lies beside the western walls of Petworth House. The local landmark here, however, is **All Hallows' Church** and, in particular its tower. Built in 1810, the tower is topped by stone pinnacles and a crown that is reminiscent of the lower stage of the Eiffel Tower. Known as a Scots Crown, the church and its tower have featured in paintings by both Turner and Constable.

Weald and Downland Open Air Museum

SINGLETON
5½ miles S of Midhurst on the A286

Lying in the folds of the South Downs, in the valley of the River Lavant, prior to the Norman invasion, this was one of the largest and wealthiest manors in England and was owned by Earl Godwin of Wessex, father of King Harold. Little remains here from Saxon times, except an ancient barn on the village green, though the 13TH century church was built on the foundations of its Saxon predecessor. Inside the church, in the south aisle, is a memorial to Thomas Johnson, a huntsman of the nearby Charlton Hunt who died in 1744. There are also two interesting monuments to two successive Earls of Arundel who died within two years of each other in the mid 16TH century.

Singleton is also the home of the **Weald and Downland Open Air Museum**. This extensive museum set in 50 acres of countryside, comprises a collection of over 40 original historic buildings, which have all been rescued from the threat of demolition and brought here to be carefully restored. Founded in 1971, the site provides an informative snapshot of the architectural heritage and rural way of life in South East England over the past 500 years. A conservation workshop has

Forge Hotel

Chilgrove, Nr Chichester, West Sussex PO18 9HX
Tel: 01243 535333 Fax: 01243 535363
e-mail: reservations@forgehotel.com
website: www.forgehotel.com

Situated just six miles north-west of the historic Cathedral City of Chichester, the **Forge Hotel** is a charmingly restored flint and brick building which has its origins as a blacksmith's cottage during the reign of Charles I. Owner and classically trained chef, Neil Rushbridger is responsible for the careful restoration and also for cooking excellent traditional English. Guests at the Forge can choose between a walk in the nearby Chilgrove Valley or a visit to the Weald & Downland Open Air Museum at Singleton – just a couple of the local attractions that are literally on the hotel's doorstep.

now been introduced and the museum hosts a programme of events which includes fine food fairs and demonstrations of rural skills and crafts such as wood carving.

For some further outdoor exploration, head for the National Trust owned **Drovers Estate**, a secret landscape of rolling farmland and attractive woodlands.

WEST DEAN GARDENS

West Dean, Chichester, West Sussex PO18 0QZ
Tel: 01243 818210 Fax: 01243 811342
e-mail: gardens@westdean.org.uk website: www.westdean.org.uk

With its sweeping lawns, punctuated by venerable trees, **West Dean** is a garden on an expansive scale. Peto's 300' foot pergola dominates the North Lawn, while in the Spring Garden, a laburnum tunnel has been reinstated and two charming summer-houses restored.

Over 20,000 bulbs have been planted in the grounds giving a spectacular display in Spring through to early summer. The Victorian Walled Kitchen Garden, one of the finest in Britain, is a must for all visitors. A 2¼ miles parkland walk offers unspoilt views of the Gardens and the surrounding countryside.

The Visitor Centre (free entry) houses a licensed restaurant and an imaginative garden shop.

WEST DEAN
6 miles S of Midhurst on the A286

Just to the south of this pretty community of flint cottages, the land rises towards the ancient hilltop site known as **The Trundle**. One of the four main Neolithic settlements in Sussex, the large site was fortified during the Iron Age, when massive circular earth ramparts and a dry ditch were constructed. Named after the Old English for wheel, the site now enjoys fine views over Chichester, Singleton and Goodwood Racecourse.

Amidst the rolling South Downs, **West Dean Gardens** (see panel above) immerses the visitor in a classic 19th century designed landscape with a highly acclaimed working walled kitchen garden containing original glasshouses and frames dating back to the 1890s. There are also 35 acres of ornamental grounds, St Roche's arboretum covering 49 acres and an extensive landscaped park to discover.

Another notable feature of the grounds is the lavishly planted 300 foot Edwardian pergola, designed by Harold Peto, which acts as a host for a variety of climbing plants.

CHILGROVE
6 miles SW of Midhurst on the B2141

To the north of this village, which is situated in a wooded valley, lies Treyford Hill where a line of five bell shaped barrows, known as the **Devil's Jump**, can be found. Dating back to the Bronze Age, these burial mounds - where the cremated remains of tribal leaders were interred in pottery urns - received their descriptive name as a result of the local superstitious habit of attributing unusual, natural features of the landscape to the work of the Devil.

WEST MARDEN
9 miles SW of Midhurst off the B2146

The largest of the four Marden hamlets all linked by quiet country lanes, West

LAUNDRY COTTAGE

Watergate, Nr West Marden, Chichester,
West Sussex, PO18 9EQ
Tel: 02392 631470

Superb self catering accommodation is available in this charming three bedroomed cottage, **Laundry Cottage**. Set in the large, converted, stone stable block around the original cobbled yard, now used as the garages for the adjacent Watergate House, the cottage has been meticulously decorated in a homely, farmhouse style, by owner, Julia Baker who is herself a farmer's wife. The rustic look in this spacious abode is supplemented by all mod cons and great attention to detail to provide all creature comforts. Colour schemes are subtle and tasteful, and there's a spiral staircase between floors.

The lounge leads out to a gravelled terrace and there's also a small walled garden in which to enjoy some al fresco drinking and dining. Watergate House estate covers a substantial 1,000 acres, and to the side of the cottage, a footpath leads to many walks, one conveniently to the nearest pub, and others further on for miles and miles out across the rambling South Downs. It doesn't take long, only about 20 minutes drive by car to visit the nearest beach at West Wittering, and the towns of Chichester and Petersfield have plenty of attractions and are just down the road.

Marden is a picturesque place much loved by artists. It is, however, the only one of the four settlements without a church. **North Marden** is home to the Norman Church of St Mary which is one of the smallest in the county, whilst **Up Marden's** minute 13TH century church, which stands on the ancient Pilgrims' Way between Winchester and Chichester is only a little bigger. Of the four Mardens, **East Marden**, is the most village like and, on the village green there is a thatched well house with a notice reading, 'Rest and be Thankful but do not Wreck me'. As the well is still very much in existence, the advice has obviously been heeded down the centuries.

COMPTON
8 miles SW of Midhurst on the B2146

A tranquil settlement of brick and flint buildings, Compton lies under the steep slope of **Telegraph Hill**. Close to the hill is a grassy mound which is in fact a Neolithic long barrow that is locally known as **Bevis' Thumb**. This mysterious burial site was named after a local giant, Bevis (the same Bevis who threw his sword from the battlements of Arundel Castle), who, as well as being very tall, had a modest weekly diet of an ox washed down with two hogsheads of beer.

SOUTH HARTING
6 miles W of Midhurst on the B2146

One of the most attractive villages of the South Downs, South Harting not only has ancient thatched cottages but also more elegant red brick Georgian houses than its neighbours. The spire of the local church is famously covered in copper shingles. Its bright verdigris hue can be seen from several miles away and acts as a signpost to this handsome setting. Outside the church stand the ancient village stocks, along with a whipping post, and inside there are several monuments including one commemorating the life of Sir Harry Fetherstonhaugh of Uppark.

Although the nearby grand house has seen many famous visitors, South Harting can boast of being the home of the novelist Anthony Trollope for the last two years of his life. Though here only a short time before his death in 1882, Trollope wrote four novels whilst in South Harting and his pen and paper knife can be seen in the church.

The village stands at the foot of National Trust owned **Harting Down**, beneath the steep scarp slope of the South Downs ridge, which is traversed by the South Downs Way. This spectacular long distance footpath and bridleway stretches for nearly 100 miles, from Winchester to Beachy Head where the path skirts around **Beacon Hill**. At 793 feet above sea level, the hill is one of the highest points on the Downs and, surrounding the summit, is a rectangular Iron Age hillfort.

Just south of the village and superbly situated on the crest of a hill lies, **Uppark**, a magnificent National Trust property. However, the climb up to the house was so steep that, when the house was offered to the Duke of Wellington after his victories in the Napoleonic Wars, he declined as he considered the drive to the mansion would require replacing his exhausted horses too frequently. The house was built in the late 1680s for Lord Grey of Werke, one of the chief instigators of the Duke of Monmouth's rebellion of 1685 and a hopeless cavalry commander who was taken prisoner at the battle of Sedgemoor. Lord Grey was let off with a fine and he retired from his none too illustrious military career and concentrated on building his house to the latest Dutch designs. As well as being a splendid house architecturally, the building of the

house on this site was only made possible with the help of a water pump invented by Lord Grey's grandfather, which brought water up to the hill top from a low lying spring.

It was a mid 18TH century owner, Sir Matthew Fetherstonhaugh, who created the lavish interiors by decorating and furnishing the rooms with rare carpets, elegant furniture and intriguing objects d'art. Dying in 1774, Sir Matthew left his estate to his 20 year old son, Sir Harry, who, with his great friend the Prince Regent, brought an altogether different atmosphere to the house. He installed his London mistress, Emma Hart (who later married Sir William Hamilton and became Lord Nelson's mistress), and carried on a life of gambling, racing and partying. However, in 1810, Sir Harry gave up his social life and, at the age of 70, he married his dairymaid, Mary Ann to the amazement and outrage of West Sussex

Uppark House

society. He died, at the age of 92, in 1846 and both Mary Ann and then her sister Frances kept the house just as it had been during Sir Harry's life for a further 50 years.

This latter era of life at Uppark would have been remembered by the young HG Wells who spent a great deal of time here as his mother worked at the house. As well as exploring the grounds and gardens laid out by the early 19TH century designer Humphry Repton, Wells had a self taught education from Uppark's vast stock of books.

Unfortunately the upper floors of the house were destroyed by fire in 1989 and, after one of the National Trust's most extensive restoration programmes, the house was reopened to the public in 1995. Luckily, most of the house's 18th century treasures were rescued from the fire and as well as having been returned to its former splendour, the fine pictures, furniture and ceramics are now on view again in an award-winning exhibition which describes the house's romantic past. Visitors can also see the famous dolls house, the rescued Grand Tour collection and explore the extensive basement servant rooms and subterranean passages left exactly as they were in 1874 when HG Wells' mother was housekeeper.

Also close to South Harting lies the site of the now demolished **Durford Abbey** - an isolated monastery founded in the 12TH century by a community of Premonstratensian monks - a strict vegetarian order founded in 1120 by St Norbert at Premontre, France. Unlike other orders of their time, which grew wealthy on the income from their monastic estates, the monks at Durford seem to have struggled for survival. In fact, so harsh was the monks' existence here that, on the monasteries dissolution in the 16TH century, is was described by a commissioner as 'The poorest abbey I have seen, far in debt and in decay.' Although little of the abbey remains today, the monks of Durford succeeded in leaving an important legacy in the form of two 15TH century bridges over the River Rother and its tributaries. (During the medieval period it was a duty of religious houses to provide and maintain such bridges.) Both Maidenmarsh Bridge, near the abbey site, and **Habin Bridge**, to the south of Rogate, are worth a visit and the latter, which consists of four semicircular arches, still carries the road to South Harting.

TROTTON
3 miles W of Midhurst on the A272

This pleasant village lies in the broad valley of the River Rother to the west of Midhurst that was once a densely wooded area known for its timber and charcoal. The impressive **Medieval Bridge** in the village dates back to the 14TH century and, still carrying modern day traffic, the money for the bridge was given by Lord Camoys, who accompanied Henry V to Agincourt. Inside the parish church is a memorial to Lord Camoys, who died in 1419, and to his second wife, Elizabeth Mortimer, the widow of Sir Henry 'Harry Hotspur' Percy. Here too, is the oldest known memorial to a woman: a floor brass of Margaret de Camoys who died in around 1310.

PULBOROUGH

This ancient settlement has grown up close to the confluence of the Rivers Arun and Rother and lies on the old Roman thoroughfare, Stane Street. It is one of the oldest inhabited sites in the district with evidence of 200,000 year old Palaelolithic camps.

Originally a staging post along the old

route between London and Chichester, Pulborough was never developed like its rival over the centuries despite its strategically important location near the rivers. It remains today a pleasant and sizeable village that is well known for its freshwater fishing. The centre of Pulborough, on the old Roman route, is now a conservation area with several fine Georgian cottages clustered around the parish church which occupies a commanding hilltop position.

Just southeast of the village lies the **RSPB Pulborough Brooks Nature Reserve** where there is a nature trail through tree lined lanes that leads to superb views overlooking the restored wet meadows of the Arun Valley.

AROUND PULBOROUGH

WISBOROUGH GREEN
5½ miles N of Pulborough on the A272

This pretty Sussex village has a large rectangular green, surrounded by horse chestnut trees, around which stand half timbered and tile hung cottages and houses. Nearby, the village **Church of St Peter ad Vincula** is particularly interesting as the original Norman building to which

the 13TH century chancel was added, has walls that are almost five feet thick and a doorway that is 13 feet high! The suggestion is that this was an Anglo Saxon keep that was later enlarged into a church as the doorway is tall enough to admit a man on horseback. During the Middle Ages, this curious church was pilgrimage centre as it contained several relics including the hair shirt, comb and bones of St James and a crucifix with a drop of the Virgin's milk set in crystal.

The village is set in the undulating country of the Weald, and to the west of Wisborough Green there are two areas of preserved woodland which give an indication to today's visitors of how most of the land north of the Downs would have looked many thousands of years ago. Looking at the countryside now, it is hard to imagine that in the 16TH and 17TH centuries this area was an important industrial centre. Thanks to the seemingly limitless supply of trees for fuel, iron foundries and forges prospered here right up until the time of the Industrial Revolution. A plentiful supply of high quality sand from the coast also led to a number of early glassworks being set up in the area. During the 16TH century, Huguenot settlers from France and the Low Countries introduced new and

THE CRICKETERS ARMS

Loxwood Road, Wisborough Green, West Sussex RH14 0DG
Tel: 01403 700369
e-mail: cricketersarms@aol.com

Deep in the heart of West Sussex, the **Cricketers Arms** sits on the Green in the beautiful country village of Wisborough Green. This popular village inn is bursting with character and olde worlde features, some dating back to the 16th century. Landlady and former accountant, Sarah Tulip made the move from number crunching to pulling pints and now attracts a loyal and broad based clientele to her well run establishment. She is passionate about food, and insists on using only the finest of fresh ingredients in their renowned cooking.

improved methods of glass manufacture and the industry flourished until the early 17TH century when lobbying by shipbuilders and iron smelters led to legislation banning the glassmakers from using timber to fire their furnaces.

LOXWOOD
8 miles N of Pulborough on the B2133

This pleasant village, which lies off the beaten track and close to the county border with Surrey, is on the **Wey and Arun Junction Canal** which opened in 1816 and linked London with the south coast. Like most British canals, the coming of the railways saw an end to the commercial usefulness of these inland waterways, and in 1871 it was closed. However, certain stretches have been restored and as well as cruising along one of the country's most attractive canals there are opportunities for strolling along the peaceful towpaths.

The village is also associated with the Christian Dependants, a religious sect founded by preacher, John Sirgood, in the 1850s. The group was nicknamed the 'Cokelers' because of its preference for cocoa over alcohol and its chapel and burial ground can be seen in Spy Lane.

WEST CHILTINGTON
3 miles E of Pulborough off the A283

Built around a crossroads in the twisting lanes of the Wealdean countryside, this neat and compact village centres on the village green which is dominated by the delightful and relatively unrestored 12th century **Church of St Mary**. Famous for its medieval wall paintings that were only discovered in 1882, this charming Norman church has an oak shingled spire and a roof of Horsham stone. Beside the churchyard gate are the old village stocks and whipping post.

COOTHAM
3 miles SE of Pulborough on the A283

The village is synonymous with **Parham**, the westernmost and the grandest of the Elizabethan mansions that was built below the northern slopes of the Downs. The estate lies just west of the village and is surrounded by a great deer park. In medieval times it belonged to the Abbey of Westminster and at the Dissolution of the Monasteries, passed into the hands of the Palmer family. As was customary, the foundation stone of the great mansion was laid by a child - Thomas Palmer - in 1577. The grandson and heir to the estate, Thomas did not fair as well as the house and he died of smallpox in 1605 after having served with both Drake and Hawkins. In the meantime, the splendid though rather dour grey stone building was constructed and, although it appears E shaped from the front, this Elizabethan mansion is actually in the form of an H as the wings project both north and south.

In 1601, Thomas Bysshop, a London lawyer, bought the estate and for the next 300 years it remained in that family. In 1922, the house and park were purchased by a son of Viscount Cowdray, Clive Pearson and in 1948, after it had been used to house evacuees during World War II the great grand parents of the present owners opened the property to the public. The splendid Elizabethan interiors have been restored to their former glory, including the magnificent 160 foot Long Gallery, Great Hall and Great Parlour, and an exceptional collection of period furniture, oriental carpets, rare needlework and fine paintings are on show.

The gardens have been restored as well, and the seven acres of wooded parkland contain a walled garden with herb beds and a Wendy House, greenhouses where plants and flowers are grown for the house, a lake and a statue garden. The house and gardens are open to the public between April and October.

STORRINGTON
3½ miles SE of Pulborough on the A283

This old market town has a jumble of architectural styles from its small heavily restored Saxon church through to the 20TH century modern concrete buildings. There is also good access from Storrington to the **South Downs Way** via Kithurst Hill. It was this beautiful surrounding countryside that inspired Francis Thompson to write his poem *Daisy* whilst he was staying in a local monastery. The composer, Arnold Bax, also lived in the area between 1940-51.

Back in the town, the heavily restored **Church of St Mary** has inside a Saxon stone coffin on which is the marble effigy of a knight who is thought to have been a crusader. When the author Dr AJ Cronin moved to the old rectory in the 1930s he used this legend as the basis for his novel *The Crusaders*.

SULLINGTON
4½ miles SE of Pulborough off the A283

This hamlet is home to a 115 foot long barn which rivals many tithe barns that were such a feature of the medieval monastic estate. An exceptional building with a braced tie beam roof, the barn, which is privately owned, can be viewed by appointment. Just outside Sullington is

PARHAM HOUSE & GARDENS

near Pulborough, West Sussex RH20 4HS
Tel: 01903 744888 website: www.parhaminsussex.co.uk
Fax: 01903 746557 e-mail: enquiries@parhaminsussex.co.uk

Idyllically situated in the heart of a medieval deer park, on the slopes of the South Downs, is **Parham** an Elizabethan manor house with a four acre walled garden and seven acres of 18th century Pleasure Grounds.

There is an important collection of paintings, furniture and needlework contained within the light, panelled rooms, including a Great Hall and Long Gallery. Each room is graced with

beautiful fresh flower arrangements, the flowers home-grown and cut fresh from the walled garden.

Open on Wednesday, Thursday, Sunday and bank holiday afternoons from April to September, and Sunday afternoons in October. Licensed lunches and cream teas, picnic area, shop and plant sales area.

Sullington Warren - owned by the National Trust this expanse of open heathland was once used for farming rabbits and now offers superb views across the South Downs.

AMBERLEY
4 miles S of Pulborough on the B2139

An attractive village of thatched cottages situated above the River Arun, whose name means 'fields yellow with buttercups', Amberley is an ancient place dating back to the days of the Saxons. Lands in this area were granted to St Wilfrid by King Cedwalla in around AD 680 and the village church of today is thought to stand on the foundations of a Saxon building constructed by St Wilfrid, the missionary who converted the South Saxons to Christianity. Later in the 12TH century, Bishop Luffa of Chichester rebuilt the church and it still has a strong

Norman appearance.

At around the same time as the church was being rebuilt, a fortified summer palace for the Bishops of Chichester was also constructed. During the late 14TH century, when there was a large threat of a French sea invasion, Bishop Rede of Chichester enlarged the summer palace and added a great curtain wall in order to protect the north side of the Arun Valley. Still more of a manor house than a true castle, **Amberley Castle** is said to have offered protection to Charles II during his flight to France in 1651. Today it is privately owned.

Amberley Museum

During the 18TH and 19TH centuries, chalk was quarried from Amberley and taken to the many lime kilns in the area. Later, large quantities of chalk were needed to supply a new industrial process which involved the high temperature firing of chalk with small amounts of clay to produce Portland cement. Situated just to the south of Amberley and on the site of an old chalk pit and limeworks is **Amberley Museum**, which concentrates on the industry of this area. Very much a working museum, which occupies a site of 36 acres, visitors can ride the length of the museum on a workman's train as well as view the comprehensive collection of narrow gauge engines, from steam to electric. The history of roads and roadmaking is also explored and, in the Electricity Hall, there is an amazing assortment of electrical items from domestic appliances to generating and supply equipment. Meanwhile, in the workshop section, there are all manner of tradesmen's shops including a

blacksmith's, pottery, boatbuilder's and a print works.

Leaving industry aside, to the north of Amberley there is a series of water meadows known as the **Amberley Wild Brooks**. Often flooded and inaccessible by car, this 30 acre conservation area and nature reserve is a haven for bird, animal and plant life. The trains running on the Arun Valley line cross the meadows on specially constructed embankments which were considered wonders of modern engineering when the line was first opened in 1863.

HARDHAM
1 mile SW of Pulborough on the A29

This tiny hamlet, on the banks of the River Arun, is home to the Saxon **Church of St Botolph** which is famous for its medieval wall paintings. Considered some of the finest in England, the paintings date from around 1100 and among the scenes on view are images of St George slaying the dragon and the Serpent tempting Adam and Eve. The murals are thought to have been worked by a team of artists based at St Pancras Priory in Lewes who were also responsible for the paintings at Coombes and Clayton.

At one time Hardham had a small Augustinian monastic house, and the site of **Hardham Priory** can be found just south of the hamlet. Now a farmhouse, the priory's cloisters have been incorporated into a flower garden. From the site, a footpath leads to the disused **Hardham Tunnel** - a channel which was built to provide a short cut for river barges wishing to avoid an eastern loop of the River Arun.

BIGNOR

5 miles SW of Pulborough off the A29

The main thoroughfares of this pretty village are arranged in an uneven square, and as well as a photogenic 15th century shop there are some charming ancient

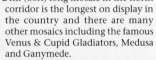

BIGNOR ROMAN VILLA

Bignor Lane, Bignor, Pulborough, West Sussex RH20 1PH
Tel/Fax: 01798 869 259
e-mail: bignorromanvilla@care4free.net

Bignor Roman Villa is situated in a superb rural setting to the north of the South Downs. Only one mile from the South Downs Way.

The mosaic floors, discovered in 1811, are some of the finest in Britain, and they are displayed under cover. The 24m (80ft) long mosaic in the north

corridor is the longest on display in the country and there are many other mosaics including the famous Venus & Cupid Gladiators, Medusa and Ganymede.

The museum, which contains many interesting artefacts found on site during excavations, tells the story of the Villa over the years. You can also see how the hypocaust under floor heating system worked.

Free car and coach parking areas, well stocked gift shop,cafeteria supplying tea, coffee and light snacks, free picnic area for visitors to the Roman Villa and facilities for the disabled are all available on site.

Guided tours and special party rates by arrangement with the curators

domestic buildings to be seen, but the main reason for visiting Bignor is to admire its Roman remains. In 1811 a ploughman working on the east side of the village unearthed a Roman mosaic floor measuring 80 ft long, which when further excavations were carried out, proved to be part of a villa built at the end of the 2nd

BIGNOR PARK

1 Bignor Park Cottages, Bignor Park, Pulborough, West Sussex RH20 1HG
Tel/Fax: 01798 869227
e-mail: info@bignorpark.co.uk
website: www.bignorpark.co.uk

At the foot of the South Downs, **Bignor Park** was originally part of the Arundel Estate, but is now privately owned. It contains two cottages and a converted barn, which are available for self catering accommodation. All three are full of charm and rustic character, but still fully equipped with all mod cons, and very child friendly. The park has many footpaths to follow, and there's a table tennis table, a hard tennis court and an outdoor swimming pool for guests' use. A little further a field are Petworth House, Arundel Castle and Wildfowl Trust and Goodwood House and Racecourse.

century AD. **Bignor Roman Villa** is one of the largest Roman villas found to date in Great Britain.

There are some 70 Roman buildings here surrounding a central courtyard. It is thought that the find was the administration centre of a large agricultural estate. The villa, being the home of a wealthy agricultural master, was extended throughout the time of the Roman occupation and the mosaic decoration of the house is some of the finest to be seen in this country.

Unlike the Roman excavations at Fishbourne, this remains a relatively undiscovered site for tourists, and, charmingly, the exposed remains are covered, not by modern day structures, but by the thatched huts that were first built to protect them in 1814. The 80 foot long mosaic along the north corridor is the longest on display in Britain and among the characters depicted on the floor are Venus, Medusa and an array of Gladiators. The **Museum** here not only houses a collection of artefacts revealed during the excavation work but there is also a display on the history of the Roman settlement and its underfloor heating system or hypocaust.

FITTLEWORTH
2½ miles W of Pulborough on the A283

An acknowledged Sussex beauty spot, the village, though now on the main Pulborough to Petworth road, has retained much of its charm which has drawn people here over the years. Well known amongst fishermen, this is a great place for the sport on either the River Rother or, further downstream, where it joins the River Arun. Others drawn here have been artists, many of whom stayed at the village inn. However, the village's most famous visitor, composer Edward Elgar, resided in a thatched cottage called **Brinkwells** in the middle of woodlands whilst in town.

First coming here in 1917, when he wrote his famous cello concerto, Elgar returned for the last time in 1921. Appropriately, the Jubilee clock in the village church has a very musical chime.

STOPHAM
1 mile NW of Pulborough off the A283

This charming place, where a handful of cottages cluster around the early Norman church, lies on the banks of the River Rother. The family home of the Barttelot family, who can trace their ancestry back to the Norman invasion, **Stopham House** is still here as is the splendid early 15TH century bridge which the family were instrumental in constructing. The impressive **Stopham Bridge** is widely regarded as the finest of its kind in Sussex and, though the tall central arch was rebuilt in 1822 to allow masted vessels to pass upstream towards the Wey and Arun Canal, the medieval structure is coping well with today's traffic without a great deal of modern intervention.

PETWORTH
5 miles NW of Pulborough on the A283

This historic town still has many elements of an ancient feudal settlement - the old centre, a great house and a wall dividing the two, and is also now an important antiques centre. Mentioned in the Domesday Book, where it appeared as *Peteorde*, this was a market town and the square is thought to have originated in the 13TH century and its street fair – one of the last remaining in the south of England - dates back to 1189 and is held annually in November. Between the 14TH and the 16TH centuries this was an important cloth weaving centre and a number of fine merchants' and landowners' houses remain from those days, including **Daintrey House** which though it has a Georgian façade, has Elizabethan features to the rear. Another house, **Leconfield**

Hall, dates from 1794 and before becoming a public hall it was the courthouse and council meeting place. Meanwhile, the garden of **Lancaster House**, close by is said to have been used as a hiding place for the church silver during the time of Cromwell.

As well as taking time to wander the streets here and see the many interesting houses, cottages and other buildings, visitors should make time to also take in the town's two museums. The **Petworth Cottage Museum** is housed in a 17TH century cottage of the Leconfield estate and that has been restored to the days of 1910 when it was the home of Maria Cummings. A seamstress at nearby Petworth House and a widow with four grown up children, the cottage recreates the gaslit setting in which she lived and includes her sewing room.

The unusual **Doll House Museum** has an interesting collection of over 100 doll's houses, inhabited by 2000 miniature people, that have been put together to create an image of present day life. Among the one twelfth size houses there are replicas of the Royal Albert Hall, a

PETWORTH HOUSE

Petworth, West Sussex GU28 OAE
Tel: 01798 342207 Fax: 01798 342963
e-mail: spesht@smtp.ntrust.org.uk
website: www.nationaltrust.org.uk

Discover the National Trust's forest collection of paintings and sculpture, as well as fore furniture and ceramics displayed in a magnificent 17'~ Century mansion with a beautiful 700 acre deer park landscaped by 'Capability' Brown. Petworth House contains works by artists such as Van Dyck, Reynolds, Titian and Turner.

Highlights of the house include the newly restored Carved Room containing Griming Gibbons' limewood carvings and landscaped by Turner and the North Gallery with over 100 paintings on display. Fascinating Servants' Quarters show the domestic side of life at Petworth. The shop, licensed restaurant and events throughout the year make Petworth a great day out.

prison and a museum full of tourists.

However, what brings most visitors to Petworth is the grand estate of **Petworth House** (see panel above) that is now in the hands of the National Trust. Built between 1688 and 1696, on the site of a medieval manor house given to the Percy family by Charles Seymour, the 6TH Duke of Somerset, Petworth House is a simple and elegant building that looks more like a French château than an English country house, and both French and English architects have been suggested. The

PETWORTH TANDOORI VICE REGAL LODGE

East Street, Petworth, West Sussex GU28 0AB
Tel: 01798 343217/343259

Run by brothers from Pakistan, the **Petworth Tandoori** is an
authentic Indian restaurant housed in a quaint, old building in
the centre of Petworth. In total contrast to the exterior and the
traditional, wood beamed ceiling inside, the walls are awash
with vibrant reds and pinks and hung with Indian art works
and lamps. All the familiar dishes appear on the menu, as well
as a mixture of baltis and curried tikka specialities. Visitors to
Petworth can browse around the many antique centres, visit Petworth House or even take in some polo
at Cowbray Park, just a few miles away.

construction of the house was completed
by the Duke's descendant, the 2ND Earl of
Egremont, and it was he who had the
grounds and deer park landscaped by
Capability Brown in 1752.

Today, the house is home to one of the
finest art collections outside London and
in fact the finest in the National Trust with
over 300 paintings including works by
Rembrandt, Van Dyck, Holbein, Reynolds,
Gainsborough and Turner who was a
frequent visitor to the House. Other rooms
open to the public include part of Lord
and Lady Egremont's apartments, a
medieval chapel, a fascinating series of
service rooms including state-of-the-art
Victorian kitchens not to mention an
impressive staircase mural by Louis
Laguerre , carvings by Grinling Gibbons

and some superb sculptures.

If your visit to Petworth happens to be
in May, it is worth checking the dates of
the Petworth Park Craft Fair, which is a
major event in the South of England. The
Petworth Festival in July also draws the
crowds with its mix of jazz and classical
music, art, exhibitions and lectures.

Just to the south of the estate is the
**Coultershaw Water Wheel and Beam
Pump.** Built in 1782, it was one of the
earliest pumped water systems, installed to
pipe water two miles to Petworth House.
Also in the building are a variety of smaller
water pumps and on the upper floor, a
variety of historical displays. Fully
restored and working, the wheel is set in a
pretty mill pond.

3 The West Sussex Weald

This area, to the north of the South Downs, is called a Weald, a word that is derived from the German word Wald, meaning forest. This would seem to imply an area covered in woodland, and though some areas of the great forest remain, the landscape now is one of pastures enclosed by hedgerows. From the Middle Ages onwards until the time of the Industrial Revolution, the area was very much associated with iron working, and to a lesser degree, glassmaking. The trees were felled for fuel to drive the furnaces and streams were dammed to create hammer ponds. The legacy of this once prosperous industry can be seen in the wealth of elaborate buildings, and particularly in the splendid churches that were built with the profits of the industry.

Those interested in visiting historic country houses will find that this region of West Sussex has several to offer. Close to East Grinstead lies Standen, a remarkable Victorian mansion, which now it has been restored to its fomer glory, is a wonderful example of the

Steyning High Street

late 19th century Arts and Crafts Movement. The low half timber 15TH century Priest House at West Hoathly, was built as an estate office for the monks from St Pancras Priory, Lewes. Now restored, it is open to the public as a museum filled with 18TH and 19TH century furniture. Also Danny, the magnificent Elizabethan mansion at Hurstpierpoint, which holds a significant place in history as this is where Lloyd George and his war cabinet drew up the terms of the armistice to end World War I.

Near Ardingly lies Wakehurst Place, a striking Elizabethan mansion built by the Culpeper family in 1590. Now leased to the Royal Botanical Gardens at Kew, the magnificent collection of trees and shrubs in the grounds are well worth seeing. Other great gardens in this region of West Sussex, include Leonardslee at Lower Beeding which was laid out in the late 19TH century by Sir Edmund Loder, and Hymans which was created with the help of the 19TH century gardening revivalists William Robinson and Gertrude Jekyll.

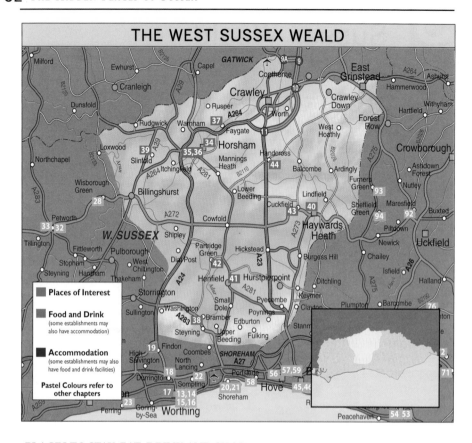

PLACES TO STAY, EAT, DRINK AND SHOP

HORSHAM

This ancient town, which takes its name from a Saxon term meaning 'horse pasture', was founded in the mid 10TH century. Some 300 years later, Horsham had grown into a prosperous borough and market town which was considered important enough to send two members to the new Parliament established in 1295. Between 1306 and 1830, Horsham along with Lewes and Chichester, took it in turns to hold the county assizes. During the weeks when the court was held in Horsham, large numbers of visitors descended on the town giving it a carnival atmosphere. Public executions were also held here, either on the common or on the Carfax, one of which in 1735, was of a man who refused to speak at his trial. Sentenced to death by compression, he was subjected to three hundredweight of stones placed on his chest for three days. When the man still refused to speak, the gaoler added his own weight to the man's chest and killed him outright. The **Carfax** today is a thriving pedestrianised area with a bandstand that often provides a venue for live music. Horsham's market scene is still thriving too. Saturday is the main day with several different markets all over town.

Horsham's architectural gem and one of the most painted and photographed streets in the whole of Sussex is **The Causeway**, a quiet tree lined street of old buildings that runs from the Georgian fronted town hall to the 12TH century **Church of St Mary**, where a simple tablet commemorating the life of the poet Shelley can be found - a celebrated local inhabitant. Here too can be found the gabled 16TH century Causeway House - rambling building it is now home to the **Horsham Museum**, a purpose for which its layout is ideal. This excellent museum has recreations of a Sussex farmhouse kitchen, a wheelwright's and saddler's shop, and a blacksmith's forge and, among the old prints and photographs, is an extraordinary drawing of a hard labour machine that was installed in Horsham Goal. It consisted of a long row of hand operated cranks, linked to a vast wind vane, which beat the air for no apparent purpose other than to exhaust the convicts. Concentrating on local history in particular, the collection is also varied and includes toys, costumes, 19TH century literature and aspects of town life.

To discover more about Horsham's past, take a stroll along the

HORSHAM MUSEUM

9 Causeway, Horsham, West Sussex RH12 1 HE
Tel. 01403 254959 Fax 01403 217581
website: www.museuma.horsham.gov.uk

Housed in a medieval timber framed building at the head of one of Sussex's most picturesque, tree lined streets, **Horsham Museum** offers an entertaining, informative and diverting destination. Founded over 100 years ago, Horsham Museum illustrates the rich and varied heritage of the area. Spanning time and space, from unique dinosaur bones to 1980's costume, from a Cambodian bronze Buddha, to a Canadian salmon caught by Millais, this Museum has surprises at every corner. The Museum has recently opened eight new galleries through the support of the Heritage Lottery Fund, which compliment the other 16 galleries, one walled garden, Sussex barn etc.

Horsham Museum is open 10.00am 5.00pm Monday to Saturday (except public holidays) and admission is free.

THE FORESTERS

St Leonards Road, Horsham West Sussex RH13 6EH
Tel: 01403 254458

The **Foresters** is an exceptionally pretty, picture postcard pub that resembles a country cottage, with its buttermilk walls and beautiful gardens that overflow with colour from award winning flower displays in the summer months. On the inside, the Foresters is a truly fine example of what a small, rural pub should aspire to – slate slab floors, low ceilings, cosy fire places, simple tasty food and a lively and dedicated landlady. Add to all that live music every fortnight and a barbeque area with league boules pitch in the stunning beer gardens, and it's not surprising that this is a very busy pub!

THE KINGS ARMS

64 Bishop Road, Horsham, Sussex RH12 1QN
Tel: 01403 253588
e-mail: tim.roberts@btopenworld.com
website: www.Thekingsarmshorsham.co.uk

Located in the busy town centre of Horsham, the **Kings Arms** attracts a broad cross section of customers from all walks of life. Thought to be over 500 years old, the pub is an appealing building with classic red tile roofing and old fashioned external lamps. Inside, two large open fires keep the compact lounge and the lovely adjoining snug roasting when it's cold outside. A balanced and imaginative menu has been created by young owner/chef, Tim Roberts to appeal to the varied clientele.

Riverside Walk around the town, which follows the River Arun and some of its many tributary streams and passes through some of the Horsham's most historic sights. Or visit the Horsham Museum with its somewhat unusual home. The roof was made 100 million years ago along a lake shore dominated by dinosaurs, while its main walls were built from oak taken from the dragon-lurking forest!

Just two miles southwest of Horsham lies the famous **Christ's Hospital School**, a Bluecoat school for boys that was founded in London in 1552 by Edward VI. The school moved to Horsham in 1902 and the present Victorian buildings incorporate some of the original London edifices. Bluecoat refers to the traditional long dark blue cloak that is still worn by the pupils, and today the school takes both boys and girls. There is also a museum in the complex, housing many old school artefacts, a portrait collection, murals by

Brangwyn and a 26.5 metre painting by Antonio Verrio. A visit here also offers the chance to see the school's marching band. All tours are guided and must be booked by appointment.

On the outskirts of town, **Owlbeech and Leechpool Woods** make a great place for a woodland walk, with large areas of Scots pine, Oak and Beech, or based around a millpond, **Warnham Nature Reserve** can be found just off the A24 and encompasses 36 hectares of natural habitat, bird hides and a visitor centre.

AROUND HORSHAM

RUSPER
3 miles N of Horsham off the A264

This secluded village of timbered cottages grew up around a 13TH century priory. However, all that remains today of Rusper

THE HOLMBUSH INN

Faygate, Sussex RH12 4SH
Tel/Fax: 01293 851539

For those seeking the passion of Italy in traditional English surroundings, the **Holmbush Inn** is the place to come. Accomplished Italian chef, Tony Mancuso presides over this imposing, late 19th century inn with his English Rose wife. Food, served in the large adjoining restaurant, is understandably Italian based, but combined with a mixture of other international influences and fresh, local ingredients. Situated just north of Horsham beside the A24, the Holmbush attracts a mixture of well healed locals and regulars who travel to the pub from surrounding counties.

Rusper Church

Priory is the church where a prioress and four sisters are buried. Although the church has a medieval tower, this is all that is left of the original building as the rest was rebuilt in the mid 19TH century by the Broadwater family. The family's wealth came from their piano manufacturing business and Lucy Broadwater (who died in 1929), to whom there is a memorial tablet in the church, was a leading figure in the revival of English folk music.

GATWICK AIRPORT
7½ miles NE of Horsham off the A23

The airport opened to commercial air traffic in 1936 when the first passengers took off for Paris. The return fare was 45 shillings (£4.25) and this included the return first class rail fare from Victoria Station, London to the airport. A month later the airport was officially opened by the Secretary of State for Air. At the same time he opened the world's first circular air terminal here which was immediately christened the Beehive. During World War II, Gatwick like all other British airports was put under military control, and amongst other uses it was one of the bases for the D-Day operations.

After the war, the terminal buildings were extended and in 1958 the new airport was reopened. Amongst Gatwick Airport's other notable firsts was the pier leading from the terminal to the aircraft stands giving passengers direct access to the planes, and Gatwick was also the first airport in the world to combine air, rail and road travel under one roof. Further extensions have increased the airport's capacity to a point where now it can handle 30 million passengers a year.

Gatwick Airport Skyview gives visitors the chance to see behind the scenes of this busy airport through its multimedia theatre, and aircraft and cockpit to explore.

CRAWLEY
6½ miles NE of Horsham on the A23

One of the original new towns created after the New Towns Act of 1946, Crawley is really an amalgamation of the villages of Three Bridges and Ifield with the small market town of Crawley. Though much has been lost under new developments, Crawley probably dates back to Saxon times though it remained a quiet and

Buchan Country Park, Crawley

unassuming place until the late 18TH century. A convenient distance from both London and Brighton, it was used by the Prince Regent and his friends as a stop over point as they commuted between the south coast resort and the metropolis. However, the coming of the railways took away the need for a resting place and Crawley returned to its quiet life. Fortunately, the aptly named George Hotel, a low coaching inn, has survived and can be found in what remains of the original centre of Crawley.

For a tranquil retreat from urban bustle, the **Buchan Country Park** covering 69 hectares of woodland and ponds is the place to head for.

MANNINGS HEATH
2 miles SE of Horsham on the A281

Just north of the village lies **St Leonard's Forest**, one of the few wooded heathland areas to survive the long term ravages of the timber fuelled iron industry of the Weald. Rising in places to around 500 feet, the forest lies on the undulating sandstone ridge that is bounded by Horsham, Crawley and Handcross. According to local folklore, St Leonard's Forest is the home of the legendary nine foot dragon which roamed the heath and terrorised the surrounding villages. Coincidentally, the bones of a prehistoric iguanodon have since been discovered in the forest by the Sussex based geologist, Dr Gideon Mantell.

LOWER BEEDING
3 miles SE of Horsham on the B2110

The name of the village, along with that of Upper Beeding to the south, is rather confusing. Lower Beeding is actually situated on the summit of a hill whilst Upper Beeding lies in one of the lowest parts of West Sussex! However, this can be explained by looking at the derivation of the shared name. Beeding is derived from the Old English 'Beadingas' which means 'Beada's people' and the Upper and Lower refer to the importance, rather than the geographical positions of the two settlements.

Just to the south of the village lie the beautiful **Leonardslee Gardens**, in a natural valley incorporating 97 hectares and seven lakes, created by a tributary of the River Adur. Laid out by Sir Edmund Loder who began his task in 1889, the gardens are still maintained by the family and are world famous for their spring displays of azaleas, magnolias and rhododendrons. Wallabies live semi wild in parts of the valley and

Leonardslee Gardens

deer and wildfowl live in the gardens. The Bonsai exhibition is a fine demonstration of this living art form, and the Loder family collection of Victorian motor cars and Behind the Dolls House – a miniature country estate of 100 years ago - are also both very interesting.

COWFOLD
4 miles SE of Horsham on the A272

This picturesque village of cottages clustered around the parish **Church of St Peter** is home to one of the most famous brasses in Sussex. Dating back to the 15TH century, the life size brass is of Thomas Nelond, Prior of Lewes in the 1420s, and along with its elaborate canopy is over 10 feet long.

Looking at Cowfold today it is hard to believe that it was once an important centre of the iron industry. The abundance of timber for fuel and reliable streams to drive the bellows and heavy hammers made this an active iron smelting area from medieval times through to the end of the 18TH century. In order to secure a steady supply of water to these early foundries, small rivers were dammed to form mill or hammer ponds and a number of disused examples can still be found in the surrounding area.

Leonardslee Gardens

Just to the south of Cowfold and rising above the trees is the spire of **St Hugh's Charterhouse**, the only Carthusian monastery in Britain. Founded in the 1870s, after the order had been driven out of France, the 30 or so monks of this contemplative order still live cut off from the rest of the world behind the high stone walls. Each monk has his own cell, or hermitage, that is complete with its own garden and workshop. The monks only emerge from their solitude for services and dinner on Sunday, and although the monastery is closed to the public, it is still worth admiring the architecture from the outside.

UPPER BEEDING
13 miles S of Horsham off the A2037

A sprawling village of cottages along the banks of the River Adur during the Middle Ages, Upper Beeding was the home of Sele Priory, a Benedictine religious house founded in the late 11th century by William de Braose. Long since destroyed, the site of the priory is now occupied by a private house. However, the French château style nunnery of **Sacred Heart Towers** is still standing but can only be viewed from the outside.

Though a quiet place today, Upper Breeding was on the route of an important turnpike road in the early 19th century and the old village toll house, one of the last in the county to remain in service, is now an exhibit at the Weald and Downland Museum, Singleton.

BRAMBER
13 miles S of Horsham on the A283

Visitors seeing Bramber for the first time will find it hard to imagine that this small, compact village was once a busy port on the River Adur estuary during Norman times, but its demise came as the river silted up. The name Bramber is derived from the Saxon 'Brymmburh' meaning

fortified hill, and after being given land here by William the Conqueror, William de Braose built his castle on the steep hill above the village probably on the foundations of a previous Saxon stronghold. Completed in 1090, the castle comprised a gatehouse and a number of domestic buildings surrounded by a curtain wall. An important stronghold whilst the port was active, the castle was visited by both King John and Edward I. Having survived the Middle Ages, the castle did not survive the Civil War, and though first held by the Royalists, it was all but demolished by the Parliamentarians. Today, the stark remains of **Bramber Castle** can be seen on the hilltop and the site is owned by English Heritage.

During the 15th century, the lands of the de Braose family were transferred to William Waynflete, the then Bishop of Winchester and founder of Magdalen College, Oxford. It was Waynflete who was responsible for constructing **St Mary's House** in 1470 - a striking medieval residence that was first built as a home for four monks who were bridge wardens of the important crossing here over the River Adur. Now a Grade I listed building, this is a classic half timbered dwelling with fine wood paneled rooms, Elizabethan trompe l'œil paintings and medieval shuttered windows. However, large though the building is, what remains today is only half of the original construction, which also acted in its day as a resting place for pilgrims traveling to Chichester or Canterbury.

Following the Dissolution of the Monasteries, the house came into private ownership and was refurbished as a comfortable residence for a well-to-do family. The Painted Room was decorated for a visit by Queen Elizabeth I in 1585, and the room in which Charles II rested before fleeing to Shoreham and then France is known as the King's Room.

ST. MARY'S HOUSE AND GARDENS

Bramber, West Sussex BN44 3WE
Tel/Fax: 01903 816205
e-mail: stmaryshouse@btinternet.com

This enchanting medieval timber framed house is situated in the award winning downland village of Bramber. The fine panelled rooms of **St. Mary's**, which include the famous 'King's Room', associated with the escape of Charles H in 1651, and the unique 'Painted Room' with its intriguing *trompe Poeil* murals, give an air of tranquillity and timelessness. On open afternoons, visitors may wander history at their leisure, helped by friendly stewards. The informative guided tours for prearranged groups tell of fact and legend from earlier Knights Templar foundations to the present day.

Once the home of the real Algernon and Gwendolen so brilliantly portrayed by Oscar Wilde in his scintillating comedy, *The Importance of Being Earnest,* St. Mary's is said to be the setting for the Sherlock Holmes story, *The Musgrave Ritual,* and has served as a location for a number of television series, including the world famous Dr. Who. The well known entertainer, Donald Swann, who gave a number of concerts in the Victorian Music Room has family connections with the house.

The formal gardens, with amusing topiary, include an exceptional example of the 'Living Fossil' tree, *Gingko biloba,* and a mysterious ivy clad 'Monks' Walk'. In the 'Secret Garden' can still be seen the original Victorian fruit wall, potting shed, circular orchard, and woodland walk.

St. Mary's is a house of fascination and mystery. Many thousands of visitors have admired its picturesque charm, and enjoyed its atmosphere of atmosphere of friendliness and welcome, qualities which make it a visit to remember.

to the public together with its pleasant gardens dotted with amusing animal topiary.

Finally, before the Reform Act of 1832 swept away the rotten boroughs, this tiny constituency returned two members to Parliament. This was despite the fact that at one time Bramber only had 32 eligible voters! One Member of Parliament who benefited from the unreformed system was William Wilberforce who was more or less awarded one of the Bramber seats in recognition of his campaigning work against slavery.

STEYNING
13 miles S of Horsham off the A283

This ancient market town, whose High Street closely follows the line of the South Downs that are hidden behind it, was founded in the 8TH century by St Cuthman. An early Celtic Christian, Cuthman traveled from Wessex eastwards

Lovingly restored and with charming topiary gardens, the house is the setting for the Sherlock Holmes story The Musgrave Ritual and it has also featured in the Dr Who television series. The house is still lived in today, but is nevertheless open

pushing his invalid mother in a handcart. On reaching Steyning, the wheel on the handcart broke as they passed Penfolds Field and the nearby haymakers laughed and jeered as the old lady was thrown to the ground. St Cuthman cursed the field

Steyning Church

and the unhelpful haymakers, and the heavens are said to have opened and torrential rain poured and spoilt their labours. To this day, it is said to rain whenever Penfolds Field is being mown. St Cuthman took his calamity as a sign that he should settle here and he built a timber church where Ethelwulf, the father of King Alfred, is believed to have been buried.

By the late Saxon period Steyning had grown to become an important port on the then navigable River Adur, and as well as being a royal manor owned by Alfred the Great it also had a Royal Mint. By 1100, the silting of the river had caused the harbour to close but, fortunately the town was well established and could continue as a market place. Designated a conservation area, there are over 125 medieval and Tudor buildings of

architectural and historical interest in the town's ancient centre. There are also several 14TH and 15TH century hall type houses as well as Wealden cottages, but the most impressive building is the famous **Old Grammar School** which was built in the 15TH century as the home of a religious order. An excellent place to discover Steyning's past is at **Steyning Museum** in Church Street where there are exhibitions showing both the town's history and some local prehistoric finds.

Steyning's close proximity to the South Downs Way and the **Downs Link** (a long distance bridleway which follows the course of the old railway line to Christ's Hospital near Horsham and on in to Surrey), makes this a lovely base for both walking and riding holidays.

WASHINGTON
12 miles S of Horsham off the A24

Standing at the northern end of the Findon Gap, (an ancient pass through the South Downs) Washington, despite the American connotations, has its name derived from the Saxon word for 'settlement of the family of Wassa'. A pretty place with a varied assortment of buildings, Washington stands between the chalk downland and the sandstone Weald.

Just southeast of the village, and not far from the South Downs Way, lies one of Sussex's most striking landmarks - **Chanctonbury Ring**. An Iron Age hillfort, the site is marked by a clump of beech trees that were planted in 1760 by Charles Goring who inherited the hill along with Wiston Park. Unfortunately, many of the trees suffered during the October hurricane of 1987, but enough remain to make this an eye catching sight on the horizon. Also here, **Wiston Park** - the part 16TH and part 19TH century mansion - is now leased by the Foreign Office and, though it is not open to the public, views of the house and the park can be seen from the road leading to the village church.

The countryside around Chanctonbury Ring inspired the composer John Ireland who, towards the end of his life in the 1950s, bought **Rock Mill**, a converted tower mill which lies below the hill. A plaque on the wall records that Ireland spent the happiest years of his life here before his death in 1962.

SHIPLEY
6 miles S of Horsham off the A272

As well as its unique 12th century village church, built by the Knight's Templar who were connected with the Crusades in Israel, this pleasant village also features a small disused toll house and a distinctive hammer pond, that in the 16th century would have supplied water to drive the bellows and mechanical hammers in the adjacent iron foundry. However, Shipley is perhaps best known for being the former home of the celebrated Sussex writer Hilaire Belloc. He lived at King's Land, a low rambling house on the outskirts of the village, from 1906 until his death in 1953, and appropriately enough being a lover of windmills, he had one at the bottom of his garden. Built in 1879, **Shipley Mill** is the only remaining working smock mill in Sussex and, whilst being the county's last, it is also the biggest. Open to the public on a limited basis, the mill was completely restored and returned to working order after the writer's death.

Belloc is not the only connection that Shipley has with the arts. The composer John Ireland is buried in the village churchyard that was built by the Knights Templar in 1125. The poet and traveler, Wilfrid Scawen Blunt, also lived at Shipley where he entertained celebrities of the day including Oscar Wilde, William Morris and Winston Churchill.

DIAL POST
7 miles S of Horsham on the A24

Just to the east of the village lie the stark ruins of medieval **Knepp Castle** - a fortification built by William de Braose of Bramber to defend the upper reaches of the River Adur. All that remains of the once impressive Norman keep is a solitary wall standing on top of a low mound which is surrounded by a now dry moat.

BILLINGSHURST
6½ miles SW of Horsham on the A272

This attractive small town, strung out along Roman Stane Street, was an important coaching town in the days before railways, and several good former coaching inns, including the 16TH century Olde Six Bells, can still be found in the old part of the town. The Norman parish **Church of St Mary** was heavily restored by the Victorians and since 1884 it has been the proud owner of a clock whose mechanism is a half size replica of Big Ben's.

ITCHINGFIELD
3 miles SW of Horsham off A264

The **Parish Church**, in this tiny village, has an amazing 600 year old belfry tower, the beams of which are entirely held together with oak pegs. During a restoration programme in the 1860s, workmen found a skull on one of the belfry beams and it is said to have been that of Sir Hector Maclean. A friend of the vicar of the time, Sir Hector was executed for his part in the Jacobite Rising of 1715 and, presumably, his old friend thought to keep his gruesome souvenir in a safe place. In the churchyard of this early 12TH century building is little priest's house that was built in the 15TH century as a resting place for the priest who rode from Sele Priory at Upper Beeding to pick up the parish collection.

THE RED LYON

The Street, Slinfold, West Sussex, RH13 0RR
Tel: 01403 790339 Fax: 01403 791863
website: www.theredlyon.co.uk

Initially built as a coaching inn in the 16th century, **The Red Lyon** has remained faithful to its original purpose in life of providing travellers with food, ale and a bed for the night, although perhaps today's travellers have not covered such long distances, particularly the locals! Situated in the centre of picturesque Slinfold village, this sturdy red brick inn has a large garden at the rear where parents can drink and chat whilst keeping one eye on the youngsters.

Inside old prints and decorative mirrors deck the walls. Run by brothers-in-law Kevin Weedon and Simon Markham and supported by head chef Leni Pavoni, The Red Lyon is a friendly establishment providing customers with a fine selection of real ales, guest beers and lagers, which can be congenially consumed in one of the relaxing lounge areas in front of a roaring fire. Food is served in the bar and oak panelled restaurant and ranges from freshly cut sandwiches to substantial Sunday lunches. There is a full à la carte menu and a daily fresh fish specials board. The village cricket pitch and parish church are close at hand, and attractions such as Hickstead, Leonardslee Gardens and Parham House are all within a few miles.

WARNHAM

2 miles NW of Horsham off the A24

This small and well kept village is famous as being the birthplace of the poet Percy Bysshe Shelley. He was born in 1792 at **Field Place**, a large country house just outside the village where he spent a happy childhood exploring the local countryside and playing with paper boats on the lake at the house. Famously, the young poet was cast out of the family home by his father who did not approve of his profession, and although there are many Shelley family memorials in the parish church there isn't one for Percy. His ashes are buried in Rome where he died in 1822, and his heart lies in his son's tomb in Bournemouth.

Encompassing Warnham Millpond where it is said that Shelley learnt to sail as a young man, Warnham Nature Reserve covers 36 hectares and offers an appealing mix of meadows, woodland and marshes, as well as bird hides and a visitor centre.

HAYWARDS HEATH

On first appearances, Haywards Heath appears to be a modern town situated on high heathland. However, the conservation area around **Muster Green** indicates where the old settlement was originally based. A pleasant open space surrounded by trees, which is believed to take its name from the obligatory annual 17TH century custom of mustering the militia, the green was the site of a battle during the Civil War. Haywards Heath's oldest building can be found here too - the 16TH century **Sergison Arms** which takes its name from the landed family who once owned nearby Cuckfield Park.

The modern town has grown up around the railway station to which Haywards

BORDE HILL GARDEN

Balcombe Road, Haywards Heath,
West Sussex RH16 1XP
Tel: 01444 450 326
Fax: 01444 440 427
e-mail: info@bordehill.co.uk
website: www.bordehill.co.uk

You can find a real haven of peace and tranquillity at **Borde Hill Garden**, created in 1890's, where botanical interest as well as garden design and

renaissance play equally important roles. 'Linked' gardens, each with their own unique style, offer a rich variety of seasonal colours. Marvel at the spring flowering bulbs and award winning camellias, rhododendrons and azaleas in May and June. In summer, the exuberant herbaceous borders and fragrant English roses give way to a vivid blaze of autumnal colour. Extensive walks to the woods with rare trees and shrubs. Borde Hill Tudor House open for conferences, board meetings and some special events.

Heath owes its prosperity, as the two nearby villages of Lindfield and Cuckfield both refused to be on the route of the railway when the line from London to the south coast was laid in the 19TH century. Today, Haywards Heath has an attractive Victorian and Edwardian Conservation area and is a lively centre for shopping, sports and the arts.

A local attraction worth seeking out is **Borde Hill Garden** (see panel above). Created at the turn of the 19th century, the garden contains an immense diversity of plant species and is the proud winner of two prestigious awards.

AROUND HAYWARDS HEATH

LINDFIELD
1 mile NE of Haywards Heath on the B2028

This famous beauty spot is everyone's idea of the perfect English village: the wide common was once used for fairs and markets, the High Street leads up hill to the church and there are some splendid domestic buildings from traditional country cottages to elegant Georgian houses. The village is also home to **Old Place** - a small timber framed Elizabethan manor house said to have been Queen Elizabeth's country cottage - and the cottage next door is thought to have been Henry VII's hunting lodge. The 13TH century village church, as well as being on a hill top has an overly large spire, which was a particularly useful landmark in the days when the surrounding area was wooded. Beside the churchyard is **Church House**, which was originally The Tiger Inn. During the celebrations after the defeat of the Spanish Armada in 1588, the inn supplied so much strong ale to the villagers that the bellringers broke their ropes and cracked one of the church bells! The inn, along with the village's other inns, were busy coaching inns during the 18th and 19th centuries, as Lindfield was an important staging post between London and Brighton.

BALCOMBE
4 miles NE of Haywards Heath on the B2036

Surrounded by attractive woodlands and wetlands, Balcombe is a picturesque village which contains no less than 55 listed buildings including the **Balcombe Viaduct**.

Wakehurst Place

Built in 1841 by David Mocatoo who is responsible for its Italianate style and four ornamental square towers, the impressive viaduct still carries the London to Brighton railway over the Ouse Valley.

ARDINGLY
3½ miles N of Haywards Heath on the B2028

Chiefly famous for being the home of the showground for the South of England Show, Ardingly still remains a relatively unspoilt village, with a couple of 14th century buildings – a pub and St Peters church – still standing. Here too, is another of the public schools founded by the pioneering churchman Nathaniel Woodard in 1858. A large red brick building with its own squat towered chapel, **Ardingly College** is set in glorious countryside. The village church, around which the old part of Ardingly is clustered, dates from medieval times though there is much Victorian restoration work. Inside can be found various brasses to the Tudor Culpeper family, whilst outside the churchyard wall was used in 1643 as a defensive position by the men of Ardingly

against Cromwell's troops who came to take the Royalist rector.

To the west of the village, a tributary of the River Ouse has been dammed to form **Ardingly Reservoir**, a 200 acre lake which offers some excellent fishing as well as waterside walks and a nature trail.

Just north of Ardingly at the top end of the reservoir, lies **Wakehurst Place**, the Tudor home of the Culpeper family which arrived here in the 15TH century. The present house, a striking Elizabethan mansion, was built in 1590 by Edward Culpeper and the house and estate were eventually left to the National Trust in 1963 by Sir Henry Price. Over the years, but particularly during the 20TH century, the owners of Wakehurst Place have built up a splendid collection of trees and shrubs in the natural dramatic landscapes of woodlands, valleys and lakes. Now leased to the Royal Botanic Gardens at Kew, the 500 acre gardens are open to the public throughout the year and as well as the varied and magnificent display of plants, trees and shrubs, visitors can take in the exhibitions in the house on local geology, habitats and woodlands of the area. Wakehurst Place is also home to the **Millennium Seed Bank**.

WORTH
8 miles N of Haywards Heath off the B2036

For those with a particular interest in historic churches, the ancient settlement of Worth which is now all but a suburb of Crawley is well worth a visit. Considered by many to be one of England's best churches, the Saxon **Church of St Nicholas** was built between 950 and 1050, though for some reason it does not feature in the Doomsday Book. Still in use today, the church is both massive and solid, but the addition of a Victorian tower and broach spire masked its importance from a distance.

The Benedictine monastery and Roman Catholic boys' public school, **Worth Abbey**, lies to the east of Worth and was originally built as the country house of a wealthy tycoon. Paddockhurst, as it was known, was built by Robert Whitehead, a 19TH century marine engineer who invented the torpedo but the house was greatly added to by the 1ST Lord Cowdray who purchased the property from Whitehead in 1894. Using Paddockhurst as his weekend retreat, Lord Cowdray, who had amassed a fortune through civil engineering work, spend thousands of pounds on improving the house including adding painted ceilings and stained glass. After the lord's death in 1932, the house was purchased by the monks as a dependent priory of Downside Abbey, Somerset and became an independent house in 1957.

EAST GRINSTEAD
10 miles N of Haywards Heath on the A22

Situated 400 feet above sea level on a sandstone hill, this rather suburban sounding town has a rich history that dates back to the early 13TH century when East Grinstead was granted its market charter in 1221. Throughout the Middle Ages, it was an important market town as well as being a centre of the Wealden iron industry. The name, Grinstead, means 'green steading' or 'clearing in woodland' and though Ashdown Forest stands quite a few miles away today, it was once a far more extensive woodland which provided much of the fuel for the town's prosperity.

Although there is much modern building here, the High Street consists largely of 16TH century half timbered buildings and this is where the splendid **Sackville College** can be seen, set back from the road. However, this is not an educational establishment as the name might suggest, but a set of almshouses that were founded in 1609 by Richard Sackville, the Earl of Dorset. The dwellings are constructed around an attractive quadrangle and they were built for the retired workers of the Sackville estates at Buckhurst and Knole. It was here, in the warden's study that the much loved Christmas carol, *Good King Wenceslas* was written.

Built to the designs of James Wyatt, the parish **Church of St Swithin** stands on an ancient site but only dates from the late 18TH century as the previous church was declared unsafe after the tower collapsed in 1785. Beside the porch are three grave slabs in memory of Anne Tree, John Forman and Thomas Dunngate, Protestants who were burnt at the stake in East Grinstead in 1665.

Before the Reform Act of 1832, only the occupants of East Grinstead's 48 original burgage plots (long, narrow housing allotments) were eligible to vote - making this one of the county's most rotten of boroughs. As was common practice elsewhere, the local landed family, the Sackvilles, would ensure that they acquired enough votes to guarantee a comfortable majority.

The arrival of the railways in 1855 ended a period of relative decline in the town and today, East Grinstead is a flourishing place. Perhaps however, the town will always be remembered for the pioneering work carried out at the Queen Victoria Hospital during World War II. Inspired by the surgeon, Sir Archibald McIndoe, great advances in plastic and reconstructive surgery were made here to help airmen who had suffered severe burns or facial injuries. Following McIndoe's death in 1960, the **McIndoe Burns Centre** was built to further the research, and the hospital remains the centre of the Guinea Pig Club, set up for and by the early patients of the pioneering surgeon.

The **Town Museum**, housed in East Court, is a fine building that was originally constructed as a private residence in 1769. An interesting place which tells the story of the town and surrounding area, as well as the life of its inhabitants, the Greenwich Meridian passes through the town at this point giving visitors the opportunity to stand with one foot in the east and the other in the west.

To the south of East Grinstead lies **Standen**, a remarkable late Victorian country mansion that is a showpiece of the late 19th century Arts and Crafts Movement. Completed in 1894 by Philip Webb, an associate of William Morris, for a prosperous London solicitor, the construction of the house was made using a variety of traditional local building materials and Morris and Co designed the internal furnishings such as the carpets, wallpapers and textiles making it one of the finest surviving examples of the company's work in a domestic setting. Now fully restored, the house which is owned by the National Trust can be seen in all its 1920s splendor, with every detail correct right down to the original electric light fittings. In addition to the rich treasures inside, Standen also has a conservatory housing many typically Edwardian house plants, includes a croquet lawn, an orchard, a wild flower meadow, a bamboo garden, a rose garden and an innovative sculpture project set amidst the beautiful hillside garden with its glorious views over Ashdown Forest and the valley of the Upper Medway. Not far from Standen the **Bluebell Railway** offers scenic rides through the Sussex Weald to Sheffield Park, the railways headquarters, via the 1930s station at Horsted Keynes.

Also nearby is another interesting house, **Saint Hill Manor**, one of the finest sandstone buildings in the county built in 1792 by Gibbs Crawfurd, the grandfather of the man who first introduced the railway to East Grinstead in the mid 19TH century. Other owners of the house include the Maharajah of Jaipur and Mrs Neville Laskey, a generous lady who accommodated the RAF patients of Sir Archibald McIndoe. The author, Ron Hubbard, was the house's last owner and it was he who oversaw the work to restore the manor to its former glory including the Monkey Mural that was painted in 1945 by Sir Winston Churchill's nephew, John Spencer Churchill, which depicted famous people, including Churchill, as monkeys!

WEST HOATHLY
5½ miles N of Haywards Heath off the B2028

Situated high on a ridge overlooking the Weir Wood Reservoir to the northeast, this historic old settlement grew up around an ancient crossing point of two routes across the Weald. The squat towered village church was begun before the Norman Conquest and inside there are a number of iron grave slabs of the Infield family from nearby Gravetye Manor. On the south wall of the churchyard is a small brass in memory of Anne Tree, one of the 16th century East Grinstead martyrs. Lying in woodland just north of the village is Gravetye Manor, a splendid stone Elizabethan house that was built in 1598 for the Infield family - a family of wealthy, local iron masters and believed to have been part of the divorce settlement made by Henry VIII with his fourth wife Anne of Cleeves. Much later in 1884, William Robinson, the gardening correspondent of The Times, bought the house and, over the next 50 years he created the splendid gardens which in many cases follow the natural contours of this narrow valley. Today, the manor is a first class country house hotel.

However, the village's most impressive building is undoubtedly the **Priest House**, a low half timbered 15TH century

Wealden hall-house with a roof made of Horsham stone that was built as the estate office for the monks of Lewes Priory who owned the manor here. This would originally have been one vast room but, in Elizabethan times the building was altered to its present form. As recently as 1905, the building was all but a ruin. Now, however, the Priest House is a quaint and typical cottage, filled with 18TH and 19TH century furniture, set in a classic English country garden. It is now a museum belonging to the Sussex Archaeological Society, the charming furnished rooms contain many interesting articles from everyday village life.

KEYMER
5½ miles SW of Haywards Heath on the B2116

Situated between two tributaries of the River Adur, this old village was once a centre of smuggling - in 1777 over £5,000 worth of goods were seized by custom – not a bad haul at all in those days! Keymer is however, better known for its famous works that still produce handmade bricks and tiles. Surprisingly though, the double spire of Keymer's Church of St Cosmas and St Damian (patron saints of physicians and surgeons) is covered not with tiles but wooden shingles.

HURSTPIERPOINT
5½ miles SW of Haywards Heath on the B2116

Surrounded by unspoilt countryside, this pretty village, which takes its name from the Saxon for wood - *hurst* - and Pierpoint after the local landowning family, was mentioned in the Doomsday Book. The narrow High Street here is particularly attractive and contains several buildings of historical note. Along with the fine Georgian buildings, the tall village church was built to the designs of Sir Charles Barry, architect of the Houses of Parliament, in the 1840s. Another

THE WHEATSHEAF
Wheatsheaf Road, Nr Henfield, Sussex BN5 9BD
Tel: 01273 492077

If you're looking for decent, honest pub fare in simple, bright surroundings, then **The Wheatsheaf** is the place to come. An attractive building with pig pink walls and a light and airy conservatory that has been added on one side, the Wheatsheaf is set just back off the B2116 about 4km from the village of Henfield. The grassy beer garden surrounded by leafy hedgerows is the ideal place to sit and soak up the fresh and calm rural atmosphere. Food is freshly cooked and wholesome and served in equally wholesome portions, making the perfect companion to one of the pubs popular real ales.

imposing building, dominating the countryside to the north of the village, is **Hurstpierpoint College** chapel. Like nearby Lancing and Ardingly, the school was founded in the 19TH century by Nathaniel Woodard.

A good time to visit Hurstpierpoint is during the second week of July to take in the Saint Lawrence Fair, which has been held here every year since 1313.

To the south of the village lies the ancestral home of the Norman Pierpoint family. They settled here in the 11th century close to their powerful relative William de Warenne, and **Danny** was in those days a modest hunting lodge situated below the grassy mound of Woolstonbury Hill. . In the mid 15th century, the family had to flee after the then owner, Simon de Pierpoint, deliberately murdered some of his serfs and the house was burnt to the ground in retaliation. The site stood empty until, in the late 16th century Elizabeth I granted the estate to George Goring who built the impressive classic Elizabethan E shaped mansion seen today.

However, the history of Danny remains a somewhat turbulent story as Goring, a staunch Royalist, was forced to give up his splendid mansion at the end of the Civil War. It was the Campion family, coming here in the early 18TH century, who added the Queen Anne south facing façade as well as remodeling the interior by lowering the ceiling in the Great Hall and adding a grand, sweeping staircase.

Danny's finest hour came in 1918, when the Prime Minister, Lloyd George rented the house, and it was here that the terms of the armistice with Germany were drawn up to end World War I. A plaque in the Great Hall commemorates the meetings held here by Lloyd George's war cabinet, and during the time that the cabinet was here Lloyd George was known to have walked up Woolstonbury Hill to seek peace and solitude. The house also saw service during World War II when it was occupied by British and Commonwealth troops. Today, Danny is privately owned but is still open to the public, although opening times are restricted.

CLAYTON
6 miles SW of Haywards Heath on the A273

This small hamlet, which once lay on a Roman road between Droydon and Portslade, nestles right under the South Downs allowing direct access to the South Downs Way. **Clayton Church**, although a rather ordinary Saxon church from the outside, houses some renowned wall paintings dating back to c1140, which are unique in England for this period. Though the date of the art work is unknown, they are undoubtedly the work of artists from St Pancras Priory, Lewes, who were also responsible for many of the surrounding churches' wall paintings.

The settlement lies at one end of the **Clayton Railway Tunnel.** Constructed in the 1840s, it was an engineering wonder of its day and is still the longest tunnel on the London to Brighton line stretching 1 1/4 miles. Best viewed from the road bridge on the A273, the northern end of the tunnel is dominated by a large Victorian folly **Tunnel House** that was built in a grand Tudor style to house the tunnel keeper.

Dominating the skyline above Hassocks are the **Clayton Windmills** fondly referred to as Jack and Jill. The larger of the pair, Jack, is a tower mill built in 1866. It fell into disuse in the 1920s and now, devoid of sails, it has been converted to a private residence and so is not open to the public. Jill on the other hand is open to visitors, but curiously enough was moved to Clayton from Brighton where it was built as a post mill in 1821. Fully restored by volunteers, Jill ground corn again in 1986 for the first time in 80 years.

PYECOMBE
7 miles SW of Haywards Heath on the A23

This ancient village stands on a prehistoric track that runs along the South Downs from Stonehenge to Canterbury and is home to one of the smallest downland churches. This simple Norman building has a 12TH century lead font that survived the Civil War by being disguised by the parishioners in a layer of whitewash.

However, Pyecombe is renowned amongst farmers and particularly shepherds, as being the home of the best possible shepherd's crook, the **Pyecombe Hook**. It was the crook's curled end, known as the guide, that made the Pyecombe Hook so special - very efficient mechanism for catching sheep but hard to fashion. Throughout the 19TH and early 20TH centuries, the village forge turned out these world famous crooks and, though they are no longer made today, several rare examples can be seen in Worthing Museum.

POYNINGS
8 miles SW of Haywards Heath off the A281

Once an iron working village, Poynings lies in a hollow below the steep slopes of **Dyke Hill** on top of which is situated an Iron Age hillfort. Just south of Poynings, and close to the hill, is one of the South Downs greatest natural features – a steep sided ravine called **Devil's Dyke**. Local legend has it that this great cleft was dug by the Devil, who one night decided to drown the religious people of Sussex by digging a deep ditch out to the coast. Working in darkness he was half way to the sea when an old woman climbed to the top of a hill with a candle and a sieve. The light of the candle woke a nearby cockerel and his crowing alerted the Devil

who, looking up saw the candle light through the sieve and fled thinking that the sun was rising.

During Victorian times, the Devil's Dyke became a popular place from which to view the surrounding downlands and look out over the western Weald to the north and the English Channel to the south, and still today the site remains a popular place with motorists, walkers and hang gliding enthusiasts.

FULKING
9 miles SW of Haywards Heath off the A281

The layout of this pretty village, situated under the steep downland slopes, has changed little since the 16TH century when the population of sheep in the area far outweighed the number of people. Besides the aptly named ancient village inn, The Shepherd and Dog, the village also has a spring and stream, now channeled through a Victorian well house, which for centuries flowed along the road side and was used for washing (or dipping) the sheep before the annual spring sheep shearing. Shepherds would bring their flocks to Fulking in droves and after the task of washing the sheep, the shepherds would retire to the inn with their dogs for a well earned drink. The spring here provided the village with all its water until the 1950s when a mains water supply was installed.

SMALL DOLE
10 miles SW of Haywards Heath on the A2037

Just to the north of this small downland village, is **Woods Mill**, the headquarters of the Sussex Trust for Nature Conservation. As well as a nature reserve and the nature trail around the woodland, marshes and streams, the site is also home to an 18TH century watermill which houses a countryside exhibition.

EDBURTON
10 miles SW of Haywards Heath off the A2037

This tiny hamlet is named after Edburga, the grand daughter of King Alfred, who is said to have built a church here in the 10TH century. However, the present **Church of St Andrew** dates from the 13TH century and inside is one of only three lead fonts remaining in the county. Though battered and dented from the days of the Civil War, when it was used as a horse trough, the font survived being melted down for ammunition. On top of the steep downland escarpment, which rises to its highest point here, stands **Castle Ring** - a mound and ditch which are the remains of an 11TH century fort.

HENFIELD
8½ miles SW of Haywards Heath on the A281

Once an important staging post, the village not only has a couple of excellent old coaching inns but also some other fine buildings of architectural note. The church is Saxon and dates back to a charter of AD 770 though it was heavily restored in the Victorian age and only a few medieval features remain. Situated near the church, the 16TH century cottage known as the **Cat House**, is a pretty if rather eccentric building and around the eaves is a procession of wrought iron cats, with their paws outstretched as if chasing

birds. This peculiar decoration is thought to have been put up by an owner whose canary was eaten by the vicar's cat.

Using domestic objects, costumes, flint tools, paintings, photographs, and in pride of place a penny farthing bicycle made by a local man in 1887, to depict life in a rural Sussex village from medieval times, the area's history can be uncovered at the **Henfield Museum**.

CUCKFIELD
1 mile W of Haywards Heath on the A272

Pronounced *Cookfield*, this small country town dates back to Saxon times and though it would be nice to believe the name was derived from the Saxon Cucufleda meaning 'a clearing full of cuckoos', it is more likely that it means the slightly less charming, 'land surrounded by a quickset hedge'. Situated on the side of a hill, Cuckfield belonged to the Norman, William de Warenne, who had a hunting lodge and chapel here during the 11th century.

Before the new turnpike road was built in 1807, Cuckfield stood on the main route from London to the south coast and, because of this it became a busy staging post. George IV used to stop here on his way to Brighton, and in the 1780s one particular stage coach was passing through here three times a day. A horse drawn coach service was maintained from here by an American right up until the beginning

THE PARTRIDGE

Church Road, Partridge Green, Nr Horsham, Sussex RH13 8JS
Tel: 01403 710391

An imposing and well maintained building, **The Partridge** occupies a roadside location at the heart of the small village of Partridge Green, not far from Horsham. Dominated by a substantial restaurant, the interior is smartly decked out with rich drapes and heavyweight furniture and is always spotlessly clean. Capable and experienced landlady Carole Daubney and her efficient team of staff ensure that the Partridge is a fine example of a traditional English pub, including the menu of varied cuisines, which chef insists are all made using only the freshest, and where possible, locally sourced ingredients.

THE WHITE HART

South Street, Cuckfield, West Sussex RH17 5LB
Tel: 01444 413454

Built in the 15th century, the **White Hart** is an impressive
building that has retained its classic appeal both inside and
out. Situated in a busy village just west of Haywards Heath,
this fine Sussex pub has been transformed by current owner,
Andrew Felton and restored to its former glory. Visitors
can enjoy some tasty, home cooked English cuisine either
in the handsome restaurant or in the compact lounge/bar
areas every day except Monday, and if you happen to be passing on the last Sunday of the month drop
in to listen to the folk night.

of World War I when the horses were
needed for the war effort.

To the north lies Borde Hill Gardens (see
panel on page 63), a splendid typically
English garden of special botanical
interest, that has been created in some 200
acres of spectacular Sussex parkland and
woods. It was Colonel Stephenson Clarke
who, by funding plant hunting
expeditions to China, Burma, Tasmania
and the Andes, established the splendid
collection of plants and trees which are
still maintained today by the Colonel's

descendants. With carefully planted
displays that offer a blaze of colour for
most of the year and regular special events,
this garden is well worth exploring.

The story of Cuckfield's history and
surroundings can be seen through
paintings and photographs at the
Cuckfield Museum.

HANDCROSS

7 miles NW of Haywards Heath on the
B2114

This little village, which stood on the old

NYMANS GARDEN

Handcross, Haywards Heath, Sussex RH17 6EB
Tel: 01444 400321/405250 Fax: 01444 400253
e mail: Nymansgntrust.org.uk
website:
   www.nationaltrust.org.uk/regions/southem

Owned by The National Trust, Nymans Garden is
one of the great gardens of the Sussex Weald, with
rare and beautiful plants, shrubs and trees from
all over the world. features include a walled garden,
hidden sunken garden, pinetum, laurel walk and

romantic ruins. Lady Rosse's library, drawing room
and forecourt garden is also open. Woodland walks
and Wild Garden.

The location is on the B2114 at Handcross, 4½
miles south of Crawley, just off the London to
Brighton M23/A23. The garden is open from 1
Mar-3 Nov, daily except Mon & Tue but is open
bank holidays. 11am-6pm or sunset if earlier. The
house is open between 27 Mar-3 Nov, same days
as garden, last entry at 4.30pm. Between Nov and
Feb the garden opens Sats & Suns,11am-4pm.
Licensed tearoom/restaurant and shop.

London to Brighton road, is home to two glorious gardens. To the southeast lie the superb National Trust owned gardens of **Nymans** (see panel on page 71). Though much of the house that stood on this estate was destroyed by fire in 1947, the empty shell provides a dramatic backdrop to one of the county's greatest gardens. At the heart of Nymans is the round walled garden that was created with the help of the late 19TH century gardening revivalists William Robinson and Gertrude Jekyll. Elsewhere, the gardens are laid out in a series of "rooms", where visitors can walk from garden to garden taking in the old roses, the topiary, the laurel walk and the sunken garden.

Just northeast of Handcross is another smaller, though not less glorious garden, **High Beeches Gardens**. Here, in the 20 acres of enchanting woodlands and water gardens, is a collection of rare and exotic plants as well as native wild flowers in a natural meadow setting. It's worth finding out about the programme of special events too.

4 Brighton and the East Sussex Downs

This coastal area of East Sussex centres around the popular resorts of Brighton and Eastbourne. Both began life as quiet fishing villages, but developed rapidly following Royal visits at the beginning of the 19TH century. Brighton, the favoured holiday resort of the Prince Regent, is best known for its lavish Royal Pavilion - a splendid example of exotic architecture and design – and its lively, cosmopolitan lifestyle. Meanwhile, just along the coast, Eastbourne has remained a more traditional seaside town and enjoys a more leisurely pace of life. Carefully planned and laid

Brighton Beach

out by William Cavendish, the 7TH Duke of Devonshire, this genteel resort is conveniently placed to combine a stay with a visit to the spectacular chalk cliffs of Beachy Head.

Beachy Head Lighthouse

Another important centre is the county town of Lewes, which dates back to Saxon times and benefited greatly just after the Norman Conquest when both a great castle and the important St Pancras Priory were founded here by William de Warenne. A coastal village that also has links with the Norman invasion is Pevensey, which was the landing place of William, Duke of Normandy and his army.

Although many of the inland towns and villages have their roots in Saxon England they are also linked with artists and writers of the 19TH and 20TH centuries. Virginia Woolf and her husband Leonard lived at Monk's House, Rodmell, until Virginia's death in 1941 whilst her sister, Vanessa Bell, maintained her eccentric household at nearby Charleston Farmhouse in Selmeston. The Elms at Rottingdean was the home of Rudyard Kipling until his success as a novelist forced him to move to a more secluded location in 1902, and the village of Ditchling became home to a group of artists and craftsmen as well as a centre for the Arts and Crafts Movement.

BRIGHTON AND THE EAST SUSSEX DOWNS

Map legend:
- Places of Interest
- Food and Drink (some establishments may also have accommodation)
- Accommodation (some establishments may also have food and drink facilities)
- Pastel Colours refer to other chapters

PLACES TO STAY, EAT, DRINK AND SHOP

BRIGHTON

Before Dr Richard Russell of Lewes came here in the 1750s, this was an obscure little south coast fishing village called Brighthelmstone that dated back to medieval times. Dr Russell, a believer in the health benefits of sea air and water, published a dissertation on *The Use of Sea Water in Diseases of the Glands*, and set about publicising the village as a place to come to derive relief from ailments and diseases by taking the sea air, bathing and even drinking sea water. He also promoted the medicinal virtues of the mineral waters of St Ann's Well at Hove. By the time of the Prince Regent's first visit to the village at 21 years of age in 1783, it was already becoming a popular place but still remained concentrated around the old village of Brighthelmstone. The effect of royal patronage on the village was extraordinary and the village grew rapidly. By the time of the Prince's last visit to Brighton, some 47 years after his first, the place had been completely transformed.

The Prince Regent later become George IV, and was so taken with the resort that he first took a house here and, wanting a more permanent base decided to build his famous **Royal Pavilion** (see panel below). Initially a small farmhouse, which had been enlarged and added to over the years, the building was transformed in 1787 when architect Henry Holland added his neoclassical design with its dome and rotunda. The final pavilion as it stands today was created by John Nash (the architect responsible for London's Regent's Park and the Mall) between 1815 and 1822, in a magnificent Indian style. Based on a maharajah's palace, complete with minarets, onion shaped domes and pinnacles, the Royal Pavilion has been the most well known Brighton landmark for almost 200 years.

By contrast, the interior of the palace moves from the Indian subcontinent to the Far East and is one of the most lavish examples of Regency chinoiserie in the world. The detail in the decoration is astonishing, with imitation bamboo everywhere - even the kitchens have not been left untouched with their

THE ROYAL PAVILION

Brighton, East Sussex
Tel: 01273 290900
website: www.royalpavilion.brighton.co.uk

The Royal Pavilion is one of the most exotically beautiful buildings in the British Isles. Indian architecture contrasts with interiors inspired by China in this breathtaking Regency palace. Built for King George IV the Pavilion was also used by William IV and Queen Victoria. Originally a farmhouse, in 178 7 architect Henry Holland created a neo classical villa on the site. It was transformed into Indian style byJohn Nash between 1815 and 1823.

A £10 million restoration scheme has returned the palace to its full Regency splendour with lavish decorative schemes. The centrepiece of the Banqueting Room is a huge chandelier held by a silvered dragon illuminating a table laid with dazzling Regency silver gilt. The Music Room is equally stunning, with lotus-shaped lanterns hanging from a high dorned gilded ceiling.

flamboyant cast iron palm trees!

The gardens surrounding this seaside pleasure palace are also the work of John Nash's elegant designs, though one ancient oak tree is said to be the one in which Charles II hid after the Battle of Worcester. However, though this is an unlikely claim, the tree certainly predates Nash's splendidly laid out grounds. Beginning life as the Royal Pavilion's stables and once housing a riding school, **The Dome** dated 1805 is now a superb concert hall. Meanwhile another part of this complex has been converted into the **Brighton Museum and Art Gallery**. Opened in 1873, this outstanding museum houses collections that are of both national and international importance. Among the marvellous displays are art nouveau and art deco furniture, decorative art, non western art and culture, archaeology from flint axes to silver coins and paintings by both British and European masters.

The creation of the Royal Pavilion and the almost permanent residence of the Prince Regent in the resort certainly sealed Brighton's fate as a much sought after seaside location and the town rapidly expanded - westwards until it met up with Hove and eastwards to **Kemp Town** (now known for its flea market), which was laid out by Thomas Reid Kemp, a local lord of the manor in the 1820s. Perhaps, the town's other great feature, after the pavilion, is the first example of town planning to take place here - the **Royal Crescent**. Built in the late 1790s, this is a

PRESTON MANOR

Preston Drove, Brighton, East Sussex
Tel: 01273 290900

This delightful old Manor House evokes the atmosphere of an Edwardian gentry home both 'upstairs' and 'downstairs'. Dating from c.1600, rebuilt in 1738 and substantially added to in 1905, the house and its contents give a rare insight into life during the early years of the twentieth century. Explore more than twenty rooms over four floors, from the servants' quarters, kitchens and butler's pantry in the basement to the attic bedrooms and nursery on the top floor. Adjacent to Preston Park and the 13th century parish church of St Peter, the Manor also comprises walled gardens and a fascinating pets' cemetery.

discreet row of little houses which also proved a turning point as, from then on, all houses were built to face the sea rather than have their backs turned towards the coast.

For many visitors to Brighton a visit to **The Lanes** - the warren of narrow streets that represent what is left of the old village - is a must. Today, these tiny alleys are the preserve of smart boutiques and in particular antique shops, as well as some excellent restaurants. Another example of regency architecture is Brighton's Town Hall, but there are some older buildings including the **Parish Church**. Situated outside the old part of Brighton, ancient pictures show the church as an isolated building that has long since been engulfed. The key feature inside is the 12TH century drum shaped font. In the churchyard is a curious gravestone to Phoebe Hessel. Born in 1713, she served in the army as a private and, after her retirement came to Brighton where she died aged 108 in 1821.

The Roman Catholic **Church of St John** in Kemp Town holds an interesting secret. Visitors make their way here to see the last resting place of Mrs Fitzherbert who died in 1837. Maria Anne Fitzherbert, twice a widow, became secretly married to the future George IV in London in 1785 and they honeymooned in Brighton, where Mrs Fitzherbert also took a house that was said to be linked to the pavilion by an underground passage. Their marriage had to remain a secret as it was in fact illegal, being completely in breech of the Royal Marriages Act. Eventually, the Prince Regent, who could not acknowledge her publicly without renouncing the throne, broke off their affair in 1811.

Another couple of places of worship worth mentioning include St Bartholomews, built in 1872-74 and nicknamed the Ark due to its vast dimensions of over 180 feet long and 140 feet high making it four feet higher than Westminster Abbey. Also, Middle Street Synagogue which is one of the finest European synagogues of any era and has a Grade II listed interior.

Just a short distance away from the sea front lies **Preston Manor** (see panel opposite), a delightful old house that has been restored and refurbished in the style of an Edwardian gentleman's residence. Beginning life as a 13TH century manor house set within beautifully landscaped grounds, the manor was rebuilt in the 1730s and extended in 1905. Laid out on four floors, there are some 20 rooms to explore from the attics and nursery on the top floor to the servants' quarters at ground level. Within the pleasant grounds is a walled garden, a pets' cemetery and a croquet lawn.

Booth Museum of Natural History

Another lesser known place of interest in Brighton is **Stanmer Park and Rural Museum**. An excellent 200 acre country park centred around the fine early 18TH century mansion that was once the home of the Earls of Chichester. The park now also contains a large municipal nursery as well as glasshouses where flowers are grown. Meanwhile, behind Stanmer House is a unique collection of agricultural implements, including blacksmith's and wheelwright's tools. The late 17TH century well house that was designed to supply water to the house and was originally powered by oxen can be seen here too.

For those wishing to take a step back into their childhood the **Brighton Toy and Model Museum**, found under the arches of Brighton station, is the place. A fascinating display includes a model train collection and a spectacular 1930s railway layout, rare clockwork liners by Bing and Napoleon's Old Guard modeled in great detail and with armies drawn up ready for battle. The world of natural history can also be discovered in Brighton, at the **Booth Museum of Natural History**. Created by Edward Booth, a Victorian ornithologist, the museum houses his original collection of some 500 species of bird, assembled between 1865 and 1890, as well as additional displays of butterflies, fossils and animal skeletons. There is also a changing programme of temporary exhibitions and special events. **Brighton Museum** is another key place of interest, particularly after a major re-vamp of its diverse collections.

Palace Pier

Meanwhile, **The Sea Life Centre**, the world's oldest aquarium, concentrates very much on live creatures and is home to the longest underwater tunnel in Europe. The tunnel winds through a series of underwater habitats where both fresh and sea water creatures can be viewed.

Like all self respecting seaside resorts in Britain, Brighton has a pier - **Palace Pier** – open everyday to entertain and amuse its thousands of visitors. But Brighton does in fact have two piers. The **West Pier** opened in 1866 and its concert hall and theatre are still two of the best surviving Victorian and Edwardian seaside entertainment buildings. Unfortunately, the pier's popularity eventually began to decline and it was sadly closed to the public after years of neglect in 1975. But it still remains a hauntingly beautiful structure and a photographer's dream!

For those looking for more refinement, there is the **Theatre Royal**, founded in 1774, that remains one of the country's best and loveliest provincial theatres. Brighton's rich cultural life is also celebrated during three action packed weekends each year in May at the Brighton Festival, the biggest cultural extravaganza in England.

Another place not to be missed is **Brighton Marina**, just one mile east of Brighton. Europe's largest marina, it has been developed into an intriguing juxtaposition of designer retail and leisure centre with old fashioned market place holding regular craft markets and food fayres.

Naturally, Brighton also has a whole wealth of places to stay, from small bed and breakfast establishments to splendid five star hotels, and, situated side by side on the front, are two superb hotels that symbolise Victorian holiday luxury. The white painted Grand Hotel, built in the 1860s, and its neighbour, the **Metropole Hotel**, completed in 1890 but later blown apart by an IRA bomb in 1984 during the Conservative Party Conference. Several people lost their lives in the tragedy and a great many more were injured. Despite extensive damage, just under two years later the hotel was once again fully open for business with no scars to show.

AROUND BRIGHTON

DITCHLING
6 miles N of Brighton on the B2116

This historic village (there are records going back to 765), which was known as 'Diccelingas' in Saxon times, was once part of a royal estate belonging to Alfred the Great before it was passed on to Edward the Confessor and then to the Norman William de Warenne. The oldest building here, the parish Church of St Margaret of Antioch, dates from the 13TH century though detail from before the Norman Conquest can still be seen in the nave.

Close by the village green and opposite the church, stands **Wings Place**, an unusual Tudor house that is also known as Anne of Cleves' House. There is no record that the fourth wife of Henry VIII ever stayed here but she is thought to have acquired the property as part of her divorce settlement.

At the beginning of the 20TH century, this pretty village at the foot of the South Downs, became the home of a lively group of artists and craftsmen including Eric Gill, Sir Frank Brangwyn and Edward Johnston. Today it remains a thriving place with many studios and galleries dedicated to the work of the artists and craftspeople who now live here.

To the north of the village lies **Ditchling Common Country Park**, a splendid nature reserve and beauty spot, with a lake, stream and natural trail. Visitors should visit Jacob's Pos - a replica of where 18th century murderer Jacob Harris' body was once hung - as bizarrely it is said to possess healing powers! Meanwhile, south of Ditchling lies the 813 foot summit of Ditchling Beacon, the third highest point on the South Downs surrounded by the scenic **Ditchling Beacon Nature Reserve**, which takes a good hour or two to explore.

Once the site of an Iron Age hill fort and almost certainly occupied by the Romans, the beacon was used as a vantage point from which fires were lit to warn of the coming of the Spanish Armada. A magnificent place from which to view much of this area - southerly over the coast and to the north over the Weald - the beacon was given to the National Trust in memory of the owner's son who was killed during the Battle of Britain in 1940.

Visitors wanting to discover more about the locality's long and interesting history should make a point of calling in at the superb **Ditchling Museum**, which is located in the Victorian former village school. From the Iron Age, there has been evidence of settlement in this area and the museum's Attree Room shows archaeological finds from prehistoric sites nearby and remains of Roman pottery dug up to the east of the village. There is also the history of the parish church and more recently of 17TH century non-conformist worship in the village. As this remarkable village has an important place in the English Arts and Crafts movement, the museum features an important collection of work by 20TH century artists and craftsmen. Work can be seen by craftsmen including stone carver and typographer Eric Gill, calligrapher Edward Johnston, painter and poet David Jones, weaver Ethel Mairet, silversmith Dunstan Pruden and artist Frank Brangwyn. The village school itself opened in 1838 and the schoolmaster's garden is stocked with fruits, flowers and vegetables as it would have been in the days of the first schoolmaster, George Verrall. Village life at home and on the farm is shown in the schoolmaster's cottage.

If a tour around the museum leaves you inspired to purchase some of the vast array of locally made arts and crafts, then the Turner Dumbrell Workshops set in tastefully converted farm buildings, has an impressive range of silverware, jewellery, hardwood furniture, pottery and designer clothes.

PLUMPTON
6 miles NE of Brighton on the B2116

The village is divided in two: the modern Plumpton Green and the old village of Plumpton. **Plumpton Green**, to the north, grew up around the railway station and is the home to the famous National Hunt Racecourse. Spectators arriving by train should look out for the Victorian signal box which has been designated a listed building following the persistent efforts of local railway enthusiasts to preserve it.

Old Plumpton is centred around its flint built church which dates from the 12TH century. The elegant moated 18TH century **Plumpton Place** remodelled by Lutyens in the 1920s is also a ;must see if you're in town. The then owner, Edward Hudson, was a wealthy magazine proprietor who had already commissioned Lutyens to renovate his other country property, Lindisfarne Castle, off the Northumberland coast.

The site of an early Bronze Age settlement can be found up a footpath opposite the East Sussex Agricultural college, and nearby is a sandstone block which commemorates the Battle of Lewes, where Simon de Montfort defeated Henry III in 1264.

BARCOMBE
9 miles NE of Brighton off the A275

Situated on the banks of the River Ouse, which is tidal as far as this point, Barcombe is a tranquil place that was a particularly favourite picnic place with the Edwardians. As well as fishing and picnicking, artists would come here to paint the dilapidated mill buildings in this splendid Ouse Valley setting. An ancient settlement - there is evidence that the Romans were here - the village was described as having a church and three and a half mills in the Doomsday Book. The half mill was one that spanned the river and the other half was accredited to the village of Isfield.

The parish church of St Mary once lay at the heart of the village, but when the Black Death infected the area the village was decimated and those who survived rebuilt their houses a mile away to the north. There are marvellous views of the South Downs from the churchyard.

RINGMER
9½ miles NE of Brighton on the B2192

This spacious village, familiar to anyone arriving at Glyndebourne by car, is one of the earliest recorded settlements in Sussex. Though nothing remains of the Saxon church that once stood close to the village's enormous green, there has been a place of worship here for over 1000 years. The present church was built in 1884 by William Martin - the man who is said to have made the first wooden wheeled cycle in Britain - after fires in the 16TH and 19TH centuries had burnt down the previous buildings. Inside the church is a very poignant memorial to the village's cricket team. During World War I they joined up en masse to fight at the front, and of the 34 club members who went to France, tragically only six returned alive.

During the 17TH century, this rural village, in a roundabout manner, played an important part in the history of America. Two young women of the parish married men who went on to become influential figures in the birth of the United States: Guglielma Springett, the daughter of Sir William who supported Parliament during the English Civil War, went on to marry William Penn, the

THE COCK INN

Uckfield Road, Ringmer, Lewes, East Sussex, BN8 5RX
Tel: 01273 812040 website: cockpub.co.uk
(on the A26 between Lewes and Uckfield)

Owners John and Joy Garnsey have transformed **The Cock Inn** into an exciting eatery with one of the most extensive a la carte pub menus in Sussex. Served in the relatively new 40 seater restaurant – one of the few modifications made since the pub was built as a coaching inn in the 16th century – food focuses on fish and vegetarian specialities as the Garnseys know a thing or two about food having previously run a vegetarian restaurant in Brighton for 21 years. Joy now oversees the extensive menu as well as maintaining the surrounding cottage style gardens, and John hand picks and buys all of the steak and meat to ensure quality is never compromised.

Being only 10 minutes away from Glynbourne Opera, opera goers and orchestra members are frequent customers, and the Garnseys are happy to coordinate a swift turn around for pre-opera or interval diners so long as they are warned in advance. Also on the doorstep is the historic town of Lewes, and not much further away, Brighton. Behind the white washed exterior, which is splashed with brightly coloured hanging baskets and window boxes over the summer, little has changed over the years. Flag stone floors and exposed brick walls are warmed by the glow of a roaring fire that burns in the Inglenook fireplace right through from October to late May.

founder of the state of Pennsylvania; whilst Ann Sadler married John Harvard, the founder of Harvard University.

However, for all its history, Ringmer's most famous inhabitant was Timothy the tortoise. He belonged to the aunt of the 18TH century naturalist Gilbert White, and during his visits to see his aunt who lived here, White became fascinated by Timothy's activities. After his aunt's death, White continued to study the tortoise and, in *The Natural History of Selbourne* he describes the tortoise's lethargic movements. Timothy's carapace can be seen in the Natural History Museum, London.

LEWES
7 miles NE of Brighton on the A27

The county town of East Sussex, Lewes is a historic settlement that occupies a strategically important point where the River Ouse is crossed by an ancient east to west land route. Much of the town's street plan dates from Saxon times, when it was one of the Saxon capitals that was undoubtedly visited by Alfred the Great in around 890. It was also considered important enough to be allowed to mint currency. The Norman invasion in the 11TH century and William the Conqueror's success at Battle, however, really saw Lewes grow in stature.

When dividing up his new kingdom, William gave the Sussex estates to his most trusted barons because of their closeness to the English Channel, and the lands around Lewes were granted to his loyal lieutenant, William de Warenne whom he instructed to build him a castle in the Lewes area. De Warenne along with his wife Gundrara began building **Lewes Castle** (see panel on page 82) on two artificial mounds soon after the Conquest

WHITE HART HOTEL

High Street, Lewes, East Sussex, BN7 1XE
Tel: 01273 476694/474676 Fax: 01273 476695
e-mail: info@whitehartlewes.co.uk
website: www.whitehartlewes.co.uk

Set in the town centre, the **White Hart Hotel** is an elegant, 16th century period style building, with a very modern operation behind its well-maintained, historic façade. Originally home to the Pelham family, the White Hart became an important coaching house famed for its catering and election parties during the 18th century. The hotel's past is peppered with interesting episodes. In the 16th century, the wine cellars were used as the town prison during the persecution of the Protestants and many martyrs were buried in the barrel-shaped dungeon. In 1929, the hotel played its part in world history, when talks between the British Foreign Secretary and the envoy of the Soviet Republic were held there and finally a treaty was signed to agree the resumption of diplomatic relations between the two countries. Today, many of the hotel's 50 en suite rooms retain the rich character of

the White Hart's historical background with their beamed ceilings and walls, some have four poster beds, whilst others are fine examples of modern luxury. The oak panelled public rooms and traditional beamed bar also include many period features, such as a Mediaeval open log fire, and a famous Parliamentary clock. Dominated by the castle, the historic town of Lewes is

one of the few towns in the south-east which still has its own privately owned brewery, and its real ale is served in the White Hart's bars. The spacious 120 seat classical restaurant is open at to both residents and locals. Its extensive selection of traditional British dishes, prepared with a strong French influence is extremely popular and booking is essential at weekends and for special occasions. The à la carte menu includes starters such as whitebait lightly fried and served with brown bread and butter, plus a wide range of vegetarian and fish dishes,

as well as several tempting steak options like fillet of steak served with wild mushrooms, white wine and finished with cream. There is also a carvery offering an excellent value three course meal, and in addition to the restaurant, food can be eaten in the smartly decorated Victorian carvery or on the panoramic terrace at the rear of the hotel with its stunning eight mile views out over the beautiful South Downs and the Ouse Valley. Fortunately, to work off a few of those excess calories, there's even a fitness club with state of the art equipment and a heated indoor pool.

of 1066 and continued for nearly 300 years. He also founded the great Priory of St Pancras. Today, a substantial part of the castle remains, including a section of the keep and two towers dating from the 13th century. Though most of the original buildings were pulled down and the stones used for other construction work, the castle was owned during the 19th century by the Kemp family who are responsible for the elegant Georgian façade to the Barbican House which covers the building's much older timbers. Overshadowed by the Barbican Gate, the house is now home to the **Barbican House Museum** where relics found in the area, from prehistoric times through to the Middle Ages, are on display. Here too is the **Living History Museum**, with its superb scale model of Lewes set at the end of the 19th century.

Lewes Castle and Barbican House Museum

169 High Street, Lewes,
East Sussex BN7 1YE
Tel: 01273 486290
e-mail: castle@sussexpast.co.uk

William the Conqueror instructed his loyal lieutenant, William de Warenne, to build a castle in the Lewes area. Building began soon after the Conquest of 1066 and continued for nearly 300 years. Today the romantic outline of the castle dominates the town. Climb to the top and you'll see outstanding views of the river and downs. Imagine how Norman soldiers might have lived. See how the town grew around the castle.Leave yourself time to explore and understand more about the past of Lewes and enjoy the beauty of the present.

Opposite the castle, in **Barbican House Museum**, you'll find an interactive touch screen, 'A Touch of Lewes', and a sound and light show, 'The Story of Lewes Town'. Both will help you see Lewes in times gone by. Following a visit to the museum roorns, you'll leave knowing much more about the historic town and its buildings.

There are also splendid views over the town available to anyone climbing to the roof of the keep.

Meanwhile, little remains of the Priory of St Pancras that some suggest William de Warenne founded not because he was pious but because of the brutal massacre of the Saxons he had witnessed at Battle. Built on the foundations of a small Saxon church, the priory and a great deal of land were given to the abbey of Cluny in Burgundy. At its height, the priory had a church as large as Chichester Cathedral, with outbuildings to the same scale, but all were destroyed at the time of the Dissolution in the 16TH century.

Lewes Castle

THE DORSET ARMS

22 Malling Street, Lewes, Sussex BN7 2RD
Tel: 01273 477110

Built in 1602, **The Dorset Arms** doesn't appear to have been hurt by the passing years and remains a distinctive, old red brick and tile building. Located in the centre of Lewes and almost next to the famous Harvey's Brewery, the pub has a strong following and is well run by enthusiastic landlord, David Whiting and his wife Lisa. Inside the pub is extremely well decorated with quality hardwood tables and chairs and a dark, mahogany bar. A varied menu features delicious homemade pies, fresh fish and plenty of house specials.

During the 14TH century a feud developed between the 4TH Earl de Warenne and Lord Pevensey. In order to settle their differences the two met one May morning under the walls of Lewes Castle. As they fought, Lord Pevensey cornered de Warenne and as he was about to drive home his sword Lady de Warenne began to pray to St Nicholas to save his life, and vowed that should her husband be spared, her first born son would not marry until he had placed St Nicholas' belt on the tomb of the Blessed Virgin in Byzantium. At that moment Lord Pevensey slipped, and as he fell, de

Warenne drove home his sword. Years went by until the earl's eldest son, Lord Manfred, became engaged to Lady Edona, and halfway through a banquet to celebrate the 21ST anniversary of de Warenne's victory, a vision of the combat appeared to all the guests. Understanding at once that the vow must be fulfilled before their son's wedding, the earl and his wife sent Manfred to Byzantium. For over a year Lady Edona waited for him to return and, finally, his ship was sighted off Worthing. A welcoming party gathered and then, with every one watching, the ship struck a hidden rock and sank with all hands. Lady Edona, watching the ship go down, gave out a sigh and sank to the ground dead. Manfred's ship is said to be seen, each year, on the same day - May 17 - to flounder on the same hidden rock and a plinth stands in memory of Lady Edona who was buried where she fell.

Beside the priory ruins is a bronze memorial by the sculptor Enzo Plazzotti, that was commissioned to commemorate the 700TH anniversary of the **Battle of**

Southover Grange Gardens, Lewes

Lewes. Fought on Offham Hill, the Battle of Lewes took place in May 1264 between the armies of Henry III and Simon de Montfort. The night before the battle, de Montfort and his troops were said to have kept vigil in a nearby church whilst Henry III and his men had a wild and in some cases drunken evening at the castle. Whether this was the reason for the king's defeat or whether it was down to bad military tactics is open to debate.

Anne of Cleves' House

Another monument in the town is the **Martyrs' Memorial** which was erected in 1901 in rather belated memory of the 17 Protestant martyrs who were burnt to death on Lewes High Street during the reign of Catholic Mary Tudor. The mainly Protestant inhabitants of Lewes found an outlet for their resentment at this treatment after the foiling of the Gunpowder Plot, and as a result the Bonfire Celebrations which still take place here are very elaborate affairs. Whilst the original reason for the enthusiasm has gone the celebrations take on a theme that stems from ancient Celtic pagan rites when fires were doused by water which represented the passing of the seasons from summer to winter.

Like Ditchling, Lewes has an **Anne of Cleves' House**, in this case an early 16TH century Wealden hall house, which again formed part of Henry VIII's divorce settlement with his fourth wife. Also as with the house in Ditchling, it is unlikely that the queen ever set foot in the building. Today, the house is open to the public and the rooms are furnished to give visitors an idea of life in the 17TH and 18TH centuries.

As for the rest of the town, this is a place of parallel lanes and alleys that drop

NIGHTINGALES

The Avenue, Kingston, Lewes, East Sussex, BN7 3LL
Tel/Fax: 01273 475673
e-mail: nightingales@totalise.co.uk
website: www.users.totalise.co.uk/nightingales/

Expect a warm welcome at **Nightingales** from owner Jean Hudson and her black Labrador, Ben. This intimate guest house and self catering garden flat are nestled in the village of Kingston near Lewes. Nightingales is popular with walkers who can follow the footpath from the back gate to the South Downs Way. Thoughtful extras such as fresh fruit and sherry are put in the en-suite rooms and eggs for breakfast are freshly laid by Jean's black chickens. The well-equipped garden flat which opens onto a south facing garden makes the perfect choice for those who prefer to whisk up their own culinary delights.

steeply down from the High Street, and there are many interesting buildings that can be picked out including **Dr Gideon Mantell's house**, the 19TH century doctor and palaeontologist who discovered the first skeleton of an iguanodon, and Shelleys Hotel where Dr Johnson was a frequent visitor.

ISFIELD
15 miles NE of Brighton of the A26

Isfield is the home of the **Lavender Line**, a working railway museum that is also part of the former Lewes to Uckfield Railway opened in 1858. It became known as the Lavender Line because the coal merchants which used to operate from Isfield station yard were A E Lavender and Sons of Ringmer. Although the line was closed in 1969, the museum displays many small artefacts in the former goods office which is the only one known to have been restored and open to the public.

Glyndebourne

GLYNDEBOURNE
9½ miles NE of Brighton off the B2192

Glyndebourne, a part Tudor, part Victorian country house, just a mile north of Glynde village, is now the home of the world famous **Glyndebourne Opera House**. In the early 1930s, John Christie, a school master, music lover and the inheritor of the house, married the accomplished opera singer Audrey Mildmay, and as regular visitors to European music festivals, they decided to bring opera to back to England and to their friends. In the idyllic setting of their country estate, they built a modest theatre and, in 1934, Glyndebourne first opened with a

performance of Mozart's *Marriage of Figaro*. However, their scheme was not an overnight success - on the second night only six people ventured here in evening dress - but the couple persevered and, by the outbreak of World War II, they had extended the theatre to accommodate 600. Since the early 1950s, Glyndebourne has gone from strength to strength and, as well as extending the theatre further, the repertoire has also increased and now includes everything from the traditional to modern 20TH century works. Today, each summer from May to August, people flock here dressed in evening gowns to enjoy a wide range of opera in a unique setting.

GLYNDE
9½ miles NE of Brighton off the A27

Situated at the foot of Mount Caburn, this small and attractive village is home to a splendid house and an ancient church. Overlooking the South Downs, **Glynde Place** was built in 1579 for William Morley on the site of a medieval manor house from flint and Normandy stone that was brought across the Channel in barges. An undistinguished family, the only member of note was Colonel Herbert Morley, a Parliamentarian who was also one of the judges at the trial of Charles I. Fortunately for the family, Morley did not sign the king's death warrant so at the Restoration the family were able to gain his pardon from Charles II. Meanwhile, the house passed by marriage into the Trevor family and in 1743 it was inherited by the Bishop of Durham. It was Richard Trevor, who with great foresight, left the exterior of the house untouched whilst turning the interior into classical 18TH century residence. The house is still in private hands and only open on a limited number of days during the year.

At the gates to the house stands the church that was built by the bishop in 1765 to the designs of Sir Thomas Robinson. Having recently visited Italy, Robinson was very enthusiastic about Renaissance architecture and, as a result, the church has a coved rococo ceiling, box pews and a gallery.

The village is also home to the black faced Southdown sheep that were first bred here by John Ellman who lived between 1753 and 1832. A benevolent farmer, he built a school for his labourers' children, and when they married he gave the couple a pig and a cow. He even allowed the single labourers to lodge under his own roof. However, one thing Ellman would not allow was a licensed house in the village, although he did not mind if his men brewed their own beer at home!

The distinctive **Mount Caburn** to the west of Glynde,

can be reached along a footpath from the village. Many thousands of years ago, this steep sided chalk outcrop was separated from the rest of the Downs by the action of the River Glynde. This process created a mound about 500 feet in height whose natural defensive properties have not gone unnoticed over the centuries. The earthwork defences of an Iron Age hillfort can still be made out near the summit and there is evidence of an earlier Stone Age settlement.

WEST FIRLE
10 miles E of Brighton off the A27

Though the village is known as West Firle, there is no East Firle - or any other Firle in the area for that matter! A feudal village of old flint cottages at the foot of the South Downs, it is dominated by **Firle Beacon** which lies to the southeast and rises to a height of 718 feet. As one of the highest points in the area, it was used by the Admiralty for a fire beacon to warn of the approaching Spanish Armada in the 16TH century but the importance of this vantage point has long been recognised. On the summit many ancient relics have been found over the years including a Stone Age long barrow and a group of Bronze Age round barrows. There was also

West Firle

THE RAM INN

Firle, Near Lewes, East Sussex, BN8 6NS
Tel: 01273 85822
e-mail: nikwooller@raminnfirle.net
website: www.raminnfirle.net

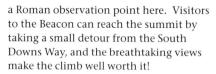

Sitting on a quiet tree lined lane in the tranquil backwater of Firle,
The Ram Inn is an attractive, unspoilt country pub that remains
relatively unchanged since it was built about 600 years ago. Family
run by the Woollers, The Ram serves traditional pub food all day
every day, as well as a special children's menu and scrumptious Sussex cream teas from 3-5.30pm. There
are two separate walled gardens, one with children's play equipment and in winter there are log fires.
The Ram is close to Glyndebourne and Charleston Farmhouse.

a Roman observation point here. Visitors
to the Beacon can reach the summit by
taking a small detour from the South
Downs Way, and the breathtaking views
make the climb well worth it!

Back in the village and set in its own
idyllic parkland is **Firle Place**, the home of
the Gage family for over 500 years. Built
by Sir John Gage the trusted counsellor of
Henry VIII and Knight of the Garter in the
15th century, this marvellous Tudor manor
house was greatly altered some 300 years
later and today it will be familiar to many
who may have seen it as a backdrop for
feature films or as a location for television
series. Still very much a family home, Firle
Place is now owned by the 8th Viscount,
and its rooms contain a wonderful

collection of both European and English
Old Masters as well as some rare and
notable examples of French and English
furniture and Sèvres porcelain. The
magnificent deer park, which surrounds
the house, was landscaped by Capability
Brown in the 18th century and it features
a castellated tower and an ornamental
lake.

RODMELL
7 miles E of Brighton off the A26

This little village of thatched cottages is
thought to have got its name from 'mill
on the road', and though no mill can be
found here today, there is a Mill Road and
in the small 12TH century church there is a
reference to its old name 'Rodmill'.

However, the village's
main claim to fame is that
it was the home of Virginia
and Leonard Woolf from
1919 until her death in
1941. The couple, escaped
the confining intellectual
world of the Bloomsbury
set in which they were
influential figures, and
settled at **Monk's House** -
a delightful early 18TH
century farmhouse that is
now in the hands of the
National Trust and open
briefly during the summer.

Firle Place

Throughout their stay here, the couple along with Duncan Grant and Vanessa Bell, filled the house with books and paintings and decorated it in a style similar to Charleston. The garden, which is lush with hollyhocks, dahlias and hydrangeas, gives good views over the downs across the River Ouse.

During her time here, Virginia wrote many of her best remembered works, but throughout her life she suffered great bouts of depression and mental illness. Finally, in 1941, she took her own life by wading into the river with her pockets full of stones. Surprisingly for the disappearance of such a well renowned figure, her body was not discovered for three weeks, and only then by some children playing on the riverbank. Her ashes, along with those of her husband who carried on living here until his death in 1969, are scattered in the garden.

SOUTHEASE
7 miles E of Brighton off the A26

This tiny village, set in a dip on the Lewes to Newhaven road, was first mentioned in a Saxon charter of 966, when King Edgar granted the church and manor here to Hyde Abbey in Winchester. Some 100 years later, at the time of the Domesday Survey, this was a flourishing village that was assessed as having 38,500 herrings as well as the usual farm produce! Inside the early 12TH century church is a copy of King Edgar's charter - the original is in the British Museum, London - and also an unusual organ that was built by Allen of Soho and installed in 1790. The only other organs of this kind that are still

believed to be in existence are in Buckingham Palace and York Minster.

TELSCOMBE
6 miles E of Brighton off the A26

Telscombe was once an important sheep rearing and race horse training centre. In fact, the last man in England to be hanged for sheep stealing in 1819 is believed to have come from the village. In 1902, the racing stables at Stud House trained the winner of the Grand National - Shannon Lass. The horse's owner, Ambrose Gorham, was so delighted with the win

Stud Farmhouse, Telscombe

that he rebuilt the village church and each Christmas gave the children of the parish a book and a pair of Wellington boots!

PIDDINGHOE
7½ miles E of Brighton off the A26

Set on a wide curve of the River Ouse, this village - whose name is pronounced 'Piddnoo' by its older inhabitants - was a great place for smugglers. Now however, the ships and boats that tie up at the quayside below the church belong to a more respectable bunch of deep sea anglers and weekend sailors! Piddinghoe is a picturesque place, with a host of 17TH century cottages and pleasant riverside walks, the golden fish weather vane on top of the church tower was referred to by Kipling as a dolphin, but it is in fact a sea trout.

NEWHAVEN
9 miles SE of Brighton on the A26

Newhaven Harbour

Newhaven itself is a relatively new settlement and it replaced the much older village of Meeching. Inhabited since the Iron Age, when a fort was built on Castle Hill, Meeching lay beside the River Ouse. However, in 1579 there was a great storm and the course of the river was diverted and its outlet to the sea moved from Seaford to near Meeching. Thus Newhaven was established at the new river mouth and it is now one of the county's two main harbours and an important cross channel port.

NEWHAVEN FORT

Fort Road, Newhaven, East Sussex BN9 9DS
Tel: 01273 517622 Fax: 01273 51205
e-mail: enquiries@newhavenfort.org.uk
website: www.newhavenfort.org.uk

Built in the 1860s to deter invaders, **Newhaven Fort** is now home to a museum that offers an insight into the sights and sounds of wartime Britain. The life-size scenes, interactive exhibitions and audio-visual presentations vividly illustrate what conditions were like for those who remained at home during World War II. Here, visitors can take a look inside Anderson and

Morrison air-raid shelters; walk through a blitzed house and experience an air-raid from inside an underground shelter.

In addition, a new World War I exhibition has been created within the fort's refurbished Officers' Quarters and, through interactive, audio-visual and film presentations, the origins of the war through to its aftermath are traced. The horrific conditions of the battlefront are also illustrated.

There is also plenty to discover outside, including underground tunnels, ramparts and cliff top guns, and children will enjoy the special Mission Trail, themed play area and souvenir shop. Special events are held throughout the year and the fort is open daily from the end of March to the beginning of November.

GARDEN OF EDEN

2 Coronation House, High Street, Newhaven,
East Sussex, BN9 9PR
Tel: 01273 515913
e-mail:Edenchadwick@aol.com

Owner Eden Chadwick aptly named this café situated in a
parade of shops on the main thoroughfare in Newhaven, the
Garden of Eden. There's room for over 50 diners inside, on
the pavement tables and in the hidden rear patio area. Food
is typical café fayre, and the all day breakfast combinations
and homemade cakes and biscuits are particularly popular.
There's also a takeaway service. Open Monday to Saturday
from 7.30 am to 4.00 pm.

Newhaven's rise began in the 19TH
century, and like many towns in Sussex, it
grew steadily busier once the rail link with
London was established in 1847. Two of
the earliest visitors to use what was then,
the passenger steamer service, to Dieppe
were the fleeing King and Queen of France,
Louis Phillippe and Marie Amelie who
stayed at the Bridge Inn in 1848 after their
sea journey before continuing to London
by train where they were met by Queen
Victoria's coach and taken to Buckingham
Palace. In order to maintain their
anonymity, the couple registered at the
inn under the rather original names of Mr
and Mrs Smith.

Also in the 19TH century, during one of
the periodic French invasion scares,
Newhaven Fort (see panel opposite) was
built. Consisting of a ring of casements
constructed around a large parade
ground, the fort was equipped
with modern guns during World
War II and also received several
direct hits from German bombs.
Today, it is a Museum where
visitors can explore the
underground tunnels and galleries
and view the permanent Home
Front exhibition. Meanwhile, the
**Newhaven Local and Maritime
Museum**, in the Paradise Family
Leisure Park, contains a wealth of
information relating to

Newhaven's port, the town's history and
its role in wartime. Also in the Park is the
Planet Earth Exhibition, which explores
the world of natural history from millions
of years ago to the present day.

PEACEHAVEN
9 miles SE of Brighton on the A259

If nearby Newhaven is a relatively new
town, Peacehaven must be considered just
a fledgling village. The brainchild of
wealthy businessman, Charles Neville, it
was planned and designed during World
War I and the intention was to call the
new town Anzac on Sea in honour of the
Australian and New Zealand troops who
were stationed here before going off to
fight in the trenches. However, after the
Armistice it was renamed Peacehaven
which very much caught the mood of the

White Cliffs, Peacehaven

Little Tea Room

55 Marine Drive, Rottingdean, East Sussex BN2 7HQ
Tel: 01273 305894

The **Little Tea Room** is an appealing spot, situated in a parade of shops on the coastal road at Rottingdean, not far from Brighton. Owner Lindsey Walton has created a delightful, country cottage style interior in pastel shades, with lace tablecothes, and an extensive collection of tea pots. Lindsey has established a name locally for her establishment and for her excellent cooking, and her homemade scones and cakes are delicious.

time, and it still remains a quiet place off the usual South Coast tourist itinerary.

Along the cliff top promenade there is a 20 foot tall monument to King George V that also marks the line of the Greenwich Meridian.

ROTTINGDEAN
3½ miles SE of Brighton on the A259

Built in a gap in the cliffs between Newhaven and Brighton, Rottingdean was naturally an ideal place for smugglers at one time. However, in more recent times, it became the home of some artistic citizens. The artist Sir Edward Burne-Jones lived here for the last 20 years of his life in the rambling **North End House** by the green. During his time in Rottingdean, Burne-Jones designed seven windows for the originally Saxon parish church that were made up by William Morris. After his death in 1898, his wife, Lady Burne-Jones maintained her high profile in Rottingdean and, in 1900, caused uproar when she hung antiwar banners from her windows following the Relief of Mafeking.

Lady Burne-Jones was also Rudyard Kipling's aunt, and he also lived in the village at **The Elms**, for five years before moving to Bateman's in 1902. Overlooking the village pond, the gardens of The Elms are

occasionally open to the public. Surrounded by old stone walls are formal rose gardens, wild and scented gardens and a wealth of rare plants. Inspired no doubt by his beautiful surroundings, he wrote *Kim* and many of the *Just So Stories* whilst residing here.

Another famous resident of Rottingdean was J Reuter - a German bank clerk, who started a pigeon post to bring back news from abroad that expanded into the internationally respected world wide news agency.

HOVE
2 miles W of Brighton on the A259

Nestling at the foot of the downs and now After some extensive changes and improvements the museum now has new galleries featuring toys, local history,

Beach Huts, Hove

changing displays of the museum's fine art collections and an interactive film gallery.

Hove is a genteel resort that is famous for its broad tree lined avenues and Regency squares, such as Brunswick and Palmeira. A former fishing village, Hove grew up alongside Brighton with the major development taking place in the early 19TH century when the seafront was built with its distinctive terraces. Hove is also home to the **Sussex County Cricket Club** and hosts teams from all over the world at their ground.

The **Hove Museum and Art Gallery** (see panel above) is housed in a Victorian villa, outside which stands the splendid wooden pavilion, Jaipur Gateway, an elegantly

HOVE MUSEUM & ART GALLERY

19 New Church Road, Hove, East Sussex BN3 4AB
Tel: 01273 290200

Hove Museum & Art Gallery is housed in a Victorian villa, built during the 1870s for John Oliver Valtance. The architect Thomas Lainson designed the house in an Italianate style made popular by Queen Victoria's Isle of Wight residence, Osbourne House. John Oliver died in 1893, but his widow continued to live in the villa until 1913. During the First World War the building was used to house German Prisoners of War and in 1923 it was converted into flats. Finally in 1926 it was purchased by the Hove Corporation for use as a museum for f:4,000. The museum opened to the public on 2 February 1927.

The new **Toy Gallery** is a magical Wizard's Attic where highlights wilt include dolls, teddies, a working train set, a workshop for broken toys and a bedroom split by time. Hove's role in the birth of cinema is explored in the new interactive **Film Gallery.** Visitors find out how film was invented through a display of working optical toys, magic lanterns and cameras. Visitors are able to learn about the Hove Pioneers of Film through displays of rare apparatus.

The story of Hove and Portslade from prehistoric times to the present day is explored in the new **Local History Gallery.** Displays feature Hove's famous prehistoric Amber Cup and investigate the Roman settlement at West Blatchington, Norman manors and churches, Hangleton's early medieval village, the Regency development of Brunswick and the growth of Victorian and twentieth century Hove.

carved structure that was transported to England from Rajashtan in 1886, and contains a whole host of exhibits on the history of the town. After some extensive changes and improvements the museum now has galleries featuring toys, local

FREE MASONS TAVERN

38-39 Western Road, Hove
East Sussex BN3 1AF
Tel: 01273 732043

Housed in a smart, Grade II listed building in a busy corner location in downtown Hove, the **Free Masons Tavern** dates back to the late 18th century and has been a pub since 1865. Its stylish interior includes ambient lighting, boarded floors and relaxing, leather sofas. An extensive menu features tasty bar snacks as well as home made daily specials with a difference, such as Swedish meatballs and Scandinavian seafood plate.

history, changing displays of the museum's fine art and furniture collections and an interactive film gallery. For history of a different kind, the **British Engineerium**, set in a restored 19th century pumping station, has all manner of engines - from steam powered to electric. Many of the model and life size displays still work and the museum's working beam engine is powered up on a regular basis.

For one of the most spectacular views of the South Downs a visit to **Foredown Tower** (see panel above) is a must. Housed in a beautifully restored Edwardian water tower, there is a viewing gallery with Sussex's only operational camera obscura and a mass of computers and countryside data that tell the story of the local flora and fauna as well as the geography of the

FOREDOWN TOWER

Foredown Road, Portslade,
East Sussex BN41 2EW
Tel: 01273 292092

Appealing to everyone with an interest in science, nature and the environment, **Foredown Tower** offers breathtaking views across the beautiful Sussex Downs, as well as interactive displays and exhibitions, countryside research and scientific data.

It is the home of the only operational camera obscura in the South East, an unusual optical device that is used to observe the landscape, sun and sky (weather permitting). The building, an Edwardian water tower built in 1909, is of archi-tectural interest and has been converted with con-siderable care to preserve many original features.

The Tower is also a popular starting point for walks on the Downs and provides details of routes and maps for walks to suit all abilities and ages.

night sky.

Also in Hove, and rather out of place with the grand Regency squares and avenues, is **West Blatchington Windmill**. Built in the 1820s and still with all its original machinery working on all five floors, the mill has been restored and continues to grind flour. As well as watching the fascinating milling process, visitors can view an exhibition of agricultural equipment.

THE NEVILLE PUBLIC HOUSE

214 Neville Road, Hove,
East Sussex BN3 7QQ
Tel: 01273 544131

The **Neville Public House,** named after a famous local family, is an imposing , brick building, located just a short walk from the centre of Hove. Outside there's plenty of off road parking and a beer garden, which doubles as a sun trap in summer. Inside, the bar area has comfy armchairs and coffee tables. Evening entertainment includes curry nights, live bands and quiz nights.

EASTBOURNE

This stylish and genteel seaside resort, which has managed to avoid both becoming too brash or disappearing into shy gentility, takes its name from the stream, or bourne, which has its course in the old reservoir in the area of open land that is now known as Motcombe Gardens. When George III sent his children here in the summer of 1780, it was, in fact, two villages, the larger of which lay a mile inland from the coast. Slowly the villages were developed and merged but it was William Cavendish, later the 7TH Duke of Devonshire, who really instigated Eastbourne's rapid growth as a resort from the 1850s onwards.

Grande Parade at Night

As much of the land belonged to the Cavendish family, the expansion was well thought out and managed agreeably which leaves, today, an elegant town, well known for its delightful gardens, that meets the demands that are laid upon it each summer. Among the first buildings that Cavendish had constructed are the handsome Regency style Burlington Hotel, St Saviour's Church, the town hall and the extremely elegant railway station. The classic pier was built in the 1880s and it remains one of the finest seaside piers in the country.

There are, however, several buildings which predate the intervention of William Cavendish. The original parish church, inland from the coast, dates from the 12th century though it stands on the site of a previous Saxon place of worship. The excellent **Towner Art Gallery and Museum** is situated in a very sensible Georgian town house that was built by Dr Henry Lushington, a vicar of Eastbourne. It became home to the town's museum in the 1920s and, as well as the collection of 19th and 20th century British art and the history of Eastbourne there are now also displays of some rare artefacts uncovered at Eastbourne's Shinewater Bronze Age site.

The story of the development of the old village into a splendid seaside resort is can be learnt at

Eastbourne Waterside

WINDSOR TAVERN

165 Langney Road, Eastbourne,
East Sussex BN22 8AH
Tel: 01323 726206

Not far from the centre of the ever popular resort of
Eastbourne, the **Windsor Tavern** sits alongside a busy
road. Formerly fishermen's cottages, the elegant, classic,
white building stands out from its neighbours in the
surrounding area. Dating back to the late 18th century,
the bulding has been a public house since the late 19th
century.

Leaseholders, Dave and Sue Harding are a local
couple who have breathed a new lease of life into the
place and established a reputation for serving quality
food and a well kept range of ales which include Abbot

Ale and a rotating guest ale. Add to this a decent range of
beers, ciders and Guiness and the choice is ample. Food is
honest, home cooked English favourites, served in a
straighforward style and very reasonably priced. Dishes
include familiar combinations like gammon and pineapple
and liver and bacon. Lighter bites and a children's menu
are also available. Food is a big thing here, and every few
weeks on a Wednesday, there's a special food themed
evening, but be sure to book a space as they are
understandably very popular. To the rear, there's a sunny
beer garden where barbeques are held on summer
weekends.

FIESTA BISTRO

6 Grove Road, Eastbourne, East Sussex BN21 4TJ
Tel: 01323 720914 Fax: 01323 646111

The **Fiesta Bistro** is a snazzy place occupying a prime
location in the centre of busy Eastbourne. Complete
with pavement tables set under an awning and a sleek
interior, it conveys a appealing continental feel. Present
owners, Ben and Mary Naderi have been in residence
since 1965 and pride themselves on the quality and
variety of their eclectic food, which includes creative
combinations like blueberry duck breast and Thai lemon
grass chicken.

MERIDALE GUEST HOUSE

91 Royal Parade, Eastbourne, East Sussex BN22 7AE
Tel: 01323 729686 Fax: 01323 419042
e-mail: cremeridale@talk21.com

Ideally situated on the seafront at Eastbourne, the **Meridale Guest
House** is a three storey Victorian property housing six well equipped
en suite rooms. The rooms vary in size, including family rooms and
some have superb sea views. Owners Terry and Chas extend a caring
and flexible attitude towards their guests, and cook up a hearty English
breakfast for them each morning. The Meridale is a place for relaxation,
yet within easy reach of Eastbourne's amenities, with easy parking and
open all year round. Children are welcome. Pets by arrangement.

the **Eastbourne Heritage Centre.**

As a coastal town during the scare of French invasions at the beginning of the 19TH century, Eastbourne had its own defences. The **Martello Tower No 73**, one of 103 built along the south coast, is also referred to as the Wish Tower. Its rather odd name comes from the Saxon word 'wisc' which means marshy place and today the tower is home to a small Puppet Museum. Another Napoleonic defence, the **Redoubt Fortress**, was built between 1804 and 1810 on the seafront. Now the home of the **Military Museum of Sussex –** the largest of its kind in the South East - the fortress houses exhibitions here that cover some 300 years of conflict on land, sea and in the air. The highlights include, relics from the charge of the Light Brigade at Balaklava, Rommel's staff car from World War II and an extensive display on the Gulf War. Other museums in the town centre include the **Musgrave Collection** of coins and artefacts, and **How we lived then** which incorporates over 100,000 exhibits from times gone by.

Eastbourne also has its fair share of greenery. On the seafront, the Carpet Gardens have a stunning example of Victorian style bedding, or visit the secluded Italian Gardens behind Holywell beach, alternatively try **Manor Park Gardens** with its driftwood sculpture, the **Sovereign Shingle Nature Park** which is crammed with more than 130 species of wild flowers or go and see the Bourne Stream from

which Eastbourne got its name in Motcombe Gardens in the Old Town.

The sea has always played an important part in the life of the town, from its early days as a fishing village and now as a resort offering a safe beach environment. Naturally the lifeboats have played an important role through the years and close to their lifeboat station, is the **RNLI Lifeboat Museum.** Here the history of the town's lifeboats, from 1853 onwards is charted through a series of interesting exhibits, including photographs of some of their most dramatic rescues.

Eastbourne has also become almost as

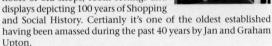

MUSEUM OF SHOPS

20 Cornfield Terrace, Eastbourne,
East Sussex BN21 4NS
Tel: 01323 737143

This famous **Museum of Shops** is in the centre of Eastbourne, just off the seafront between the War memorial roundabout and the main theatres. Visitors say this is one of the most comprehensive collections of its kind in the country as there are over 100,000 exhibits on four floors of old shops, room settings and displays depicting 100 years of Shopping and Social History. Certianly it's one of the oldest established having been amassed during the past 40 years by Jan and Graham Upton.

To the sounds of horses and carriages stroll through the Victorian styled streets, wonder at the chemist with his "cure all" preparations or remember "Five boys" chocolate. See the ironmonger, who sold everything from pot menders to mouse traps, the office or boot repairers, the draper's or tailor's and proud portraits in the photographer's. There's wind up gramaphones in

the music shop whilst the toy shop is full of childhood memories.

Mr. Barton, the grocer, is selling biscuits from glass topped tins and in the seafarer's inn the sailor is enjoying his pint. Re-live the Wartime and rationing - with the authentic kitchen/

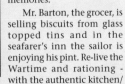

living room, complete with air raid shelter. See the Edwardian kitchen or village post office, "Christmas Past" or the jewellers and many other displays including eggcups and a huge collection of royal souvenirs.

well known now for hosting the International Ladies' Tennis Championships, held in June the week before Wimbledon at Devonshire Park as for its charm as seaside resort. Another major pull for visitors is Beachy Head. One of the most spectacular and highest chalk precipices in England, with a sheer drop of over 500 feet in places. The grand scale of the cliffs are brought home by the sight of the lighthouse, at the cliff base, which is completely dwarfed.

Eastbourne Pier

Backed by Beachy Head cliffs, Falling Sands beach is a totally unspoilt haven and ideal for a walk beside the sea.

Up on the clifftop is the **Beachy Head Countryside Centre** which focuses on downland life, from the Bronze Age onwards and includes numerous wildlife displays. This is also the end (or the beginning) of the **South Downs Way**, the long distance bridleway that was first established in 1972.

AROUND EASTBOURNE

POLEGATE
4 miles N of Eastbourne on the A27

The village grew up in the 19TH century around a railway junction and is now almost a suburb of Eastbourne. Visitors coming here generally make for the **Polegate Windmill and Museum** - a splendid red brick tower mill built in 1817 that is one of the few tower mills open to the public (though on a limited basis). Restored as early as 1867, all its internal machinery is in working order and there is also a small but fascinating museum of milling.

Though the village is relatively recent, the area has been inhabited for a long time and the remains of Otham Priory, founded in 1175, can still be seen and some of the buildings have been incorporated into a private house.

Beachy Head

RAILWAY TAVERN

17 Station Road, Hailsham, East Sussex BN27 2BH
Tel/Fax: 01323 842442

A former railway station, the **Railway Tavern** still
retains a train theme inside with many interesting
photos decorating the colourful, beamed walls.
Located in the centre of Hailsham, the pub has a
small, enclosed garden with picnic tables and a
barbeque area. Experienced publicans, James and
Val Herlihy have created a comfortable and
welcoming atmosphere, which attracts both locals
and holiday makers. Good, traditional, home
cooking rules and there's a wide range of frequently changing cask ales to imbibe.

HAILSHAM
7 miles N of Eastbourne on the A295

This market town, which first received its
charter in 1252 from Henry III, is a
pleasant town where the modern
shopping facilities sit comfortably with the
chiefly Georgian High Street. Once a
thriving centre of the rope and string
industry, Hailsham had the dubious
honour of supplying all the rope for public
executions. Now, its rope and string are
put to less lethal uses! Meanwhile, it
maintains its rural roots and the three acre
cattle market is one of the largest in Sussex
- in the 19TH century shepherds from as far
a field as Wales were known to bring their
sheep here. Several other buildings,
including the 15th century Church of St
Mary the Virgin and the Heritage Centre
(Museum) are also of historical note.

PEVENSEY
4 miles NE of Eastbourne on the A259

Situated on the coast, in the shelter of
Pevensey Bay, it was here in 1066 that
William the Conqueror landed with his
troops prior to the Battle of Hastings.
Then an important sea port, this was
where William left his half brother, Robert,
while he went off to defeat Harold, and
Visitors can follow in the Conqueror's
footsteps by following the 31 mile 1066
Country Walk from Pevensey Castle via
Battle Abbey to Rye.

Many centuries earlier, Pevensey was the
landing place for invading Roman legions
and they built a fortification here to
protect their anchorage. The fortress of
Anderida, built around AD 280, was one of
the first south coast defences and it was on
this site, that Robert built a Norman
fortress. The 11TH century stone keep was
joined in the 13TH century by a stone
curtain wall and, unlike many medieval
castles, **Pevensey Castle** seemed well able
to withstand attack. Following the Battle
of Lewes, Simon de Montfort lay siege here
and again Pevensey Castle withstood.
However, the structure gradually fell into
disrepair but it was brought back into
service briefly during the advance of the
Spanish Armada and again during World
War II. Today , the castle is capably run
by English Heritage whose free audio tour
brings the castle's history to life from its
Roman origins right up to its important
role in World War II

In the rest of the village there are an
unusually high number of fine medieval
buildings including the **Mint House**, a
14TH century building that lies outside the
castle gates. Coins have been minted on
this site since 1076 and, though it is now
an antiques showroom, visitors can see the
priest's secret room and King Edward VI's
bedroom. Any self respecting old building
has a ghost and the Mint House is no

exception. In the 1580s an Elizabethan woman, the mistress of the London merchant Thomas Dight, lived at the house and, on coming back unexpectedly, Dight found her in bed with her lover. Incensed with jealousy, Dight ordered his servants to cut out her tongue and hold her whilst she was made to watch her lover being roasted to death over a fire. The lover's body was thrown into the harbour and the mistress lead to an upstairs room where she starved to death. Another resident of the Mint House was Andrew Borde, the court physician to Henry VIII and also his unofficial jester. An interesting man, Borde was born in 1490, took orders, studied medicine in Europe and acted as a spy for Thomas Cromwell. A recognised wit of his day, his humour lead to his downfall and he died in prison after being tried on a trumped up charge by a gentleman he had satirized.

PRIORY COURT HOTEL

Castle Road, Pevensey,
East Sussex BN24 5LG
Tel: 01323 763150
Fax: 01323 769030
e-mail: info@priorycourthotel.com
website: www.priorycourthotel.com

Named after the priory that originally occupied the site, the **Priory Court Hotel** is now housed in a large, olde worlde 17th Century building. Set in well tended, landscaped gardens overlooking the walls of Pevensey Castle, its white façade is chequered with thick black beams and dotted with antique, diamond paned windows. Inside a cosy atmosphere pervades, created by beamed ceilings, oak panelling and a log burning fire. There are even a few four poster beds to add a touch of romance to your visit. Family run by the Watsons who also live in the hotel, the Priory Court offers guests a tempting menu of seasonal cuisine which can be enjoyed in the traditional bar or in the intimate, candle lit restaurant.

This charming hotel makes a perfect base for visiting Eastborne, just ten minutes away by car, and for exploring the surrounding 1066 country. The immediate area is also rich in attractions. Right next door is the Mint House, built in 1342 it is the oldest house in Pevensey. The Court House, reputed to be the smallest in England, dates back to the 6th Century and nearby Pevensey Castle, which is Roman and was constructed as a defence against Saxon Pirates, also contains a compact Norman Castle within its walls that features in the Bayeaux Tapestry. Pevensey village itself is charming and one of the historic cinque ports on the south coast, and the secluded beaches of Pevensey Bay are close at hand.

THE MOORINGS

Seaville Drive, Pevensey Bay, East Sussex BN24 6AL
Tel: 01323 761126 Fax: 01323 760738

Sitting right on the stony beach of Pevensey Bay, **The Moorings** provides customers with great sea views from the windows of its conservatory restaurant and bar. The large, Victorian pub is owned and run by husband and wife team Philip and Pamela Jacobs. As well as being literally on the beach, The Moorings makes a convenient refreshment stop after a tour of Pevensey Castle which is not far away. A sizeable wine list and locally brewed selection of cask ales contribute to the liquid refreshment, and the menu of home cooked traditional British pub fare is enhanced by plenty of fresh fish.

NAPIER HOUSE

off Collier Road, The Promenade, Pevensey Bay,
East Sussex BN24 6HD
Tel: 01323 766242 mobile: 07939 083517

Former professional dancer, Linda Gregory makes a hospitable and charming host at the **Napier House**. Set in a Victorian seafront house overlooking the beach in Pevensey Bay, this welcoming B&B has three comfortably furnished guest rooms, and guests are served an exceptional and substantial breakfast in the morning, before an invigorating stroll along the beach or drive into the nearby resort of Eastbourne.

In the days prior to the founding of the Royal Navy, Pevensey served as one of the nation's Cinque Ports - that is to say, it was granted certain privileges by the Crown in return for providing ships and men in defence of the south coast.

Pevensey used to be able to claim to have the smallest operating town hall in the country. Built in 1540, the Court House, measuring just 18 x 14 ft operated until 1886 when the tide went out and the town was no longer a port. It then became a charitable trust , and is still open to the public during the tourist season to view such relics as the oldest surviving Clinque Port Seal.

Inland, lies the area of drained marshland known as the **Pevensey Levels**. At one time this was an area of tidal mudflats which were covered in shallow salt pans: since then it has been reclaimed for agricultural use and is now covered in fertile arable fields.

WESTHAM
4 miles NE of Eastbourne on the B2191

This pretty village is home to one of the most ruggedly beautiful churches in Sussex. Dating from the 14TH century and much patched and braced over the years, the parish church houses a memorial to John Thatcher who died in 1649 and left his estate to the 'Old Brethren' in the hope that, one day, Roman Catholicism would once again be the religion of England.

EAST DEAN
3 miles W of Eastbourne off the A259

This charming village at the foot of the South Downs is one of the county's most picturesque, with its village green surrounded by a pub, flint cottages and an ancient church. Once a favourite haunt of smugglers who used to meet at the Tiger Inn - a splendid 13TH century inn that for several centuries used this name before anyone realised that the animal on the local Bardolf family's coat of arms was not a tiger but, in fact, a leopard.

Just south of the village, right on the coast, is **Birling Gap**, a huge cleft in the cliffs which offers the only access to the beach between Eastbourne and Cuckmere Haven. Naturally, this was another great place for smugglers who landed their contraband here before making their way up the steep steps to the cliff top. This stretch of the coast, during the 18TH century, was managed by a particularly notorious gang led by Stanton Collins. He had his headquarters in Alfriston and, on one particular night, the gang are said to have moved the lumps of chalk from the cliff path so that pursuing customs officers could not find their way. One unfortunate officer fell over the cliff edge but miraculously held on by his finger tips. Collins' gang came upon him and, after listening to his pleas to rescue him, they stamped on his fingers and he fell to his death.

Seven Sisters from East Dean

To the east of the gap lie the famous **Seven Sisters**, huge great blocks of chalk, the highest is 260 feet, which guard the coast between Eastbourne and Seaford.

FRISTON
3½ miles W of Eastbourne on the A259

This is more a hamlet than a village, as only a part Norman church and a Tudor manor house can be found around the village pond. The churchyard however, is interesting as it contains the grave of the composer Frank Bridge, one of the pioneers of 20TH century English music and also the teacher of Benjamin Britten. Born in Brighton, Bridge lived in Friston for much of his life though he died in Eastbourne in 1941. The south door was placed here in his memory. The village pond, too, has a claim to fame as it was the first in the country to be designated an ancient monument.

To the north and west of the village lies **Friston Forest**, 1600 acres of woodland that were planted in 1927 by the Forestry Commission. There is a circular tour through the forest so that you don't get lost!

WEST DEAN
5 miles W of Eastbourne off the A259

Though the village is only a couple of miles from the south coast and close to Eastbourne, its position, hidden among trees in a downland combe, gives an impression that it is an isolated, timeless place. King Alfred is thought to have had a palace here and kept a great fleet here on the River Cuckmere, which then formed a much deeper and wider estuary.

The village is now the home of **Charleston Manor**, an ancient house that was originally built in 1080 for William the Conqueror's cupbearer. Recorded in the Domesday Book as Cerlestone, the house has been added to over the years and it forms the centrepiece of a remarkable garden. Planted in the narrow valley, just north of Westdean's centre, the garden has more the feel of a Continental rather than an English garden with its parterres and terraces.

SEAFORD
8 miles W of Eastbourne on the A259

Once a thriving port on the River Ouse, Seaford was also a member of the confederation of Cinque Ports. Following the great storm in the 16TH century which changed the course of the River Ouse, Seaford lost its harbour and also its livelihood to the newly established Newhaven. Traces of the old medieval seafaring town can still be seen around the old church but, overshadowed by Brighton and Eastbourne on either side, the town never gained the status of its neighbours. The building of the esplanade in the 1870s did bring some development as a modest resort but the constant pounding of the sea, particularly in winter, has kept the development small.

However, during the threat of a possible French invasion in the early 19TH century, Seaford was considered important enough to be the site of the most westerly Martello Tower, which is now the **Seaford Museum of Local History** (see panel opposite, and amongst the exhibits in this lively museum are a World War II kitchen, radio sets, vintage lavatories and mementoes from shipwrecks. From the roof of the tower there are magnificent views over the town and beyond as well as the tower's original cannon.

To the west of the town lies **Seaford Head Nature Reserve**, an excellent place from which to view the Seven Sisters cliffs formed during the Great Ice Age and which still contain considerable amounts of larger fossils. Keen photographers should go to Hope Gap to take the classic shot of the Sisters as seen in tourist brochures. The nature reserve contains over 250 species of plants and supports a wealth of wildfowl on its 308 acres of mudflats, meadowland and downland.

SEAFORD MUSEUM

Martello Tower, Esplanade, Seaford, East Sussex
Tel: 01323 898222
e-mail: museumseaford@tinyonline.co.uk
website: www.seafordmuseum.org

The **Seaford Museum of Local History** is located on the stormy seafront in the last of the chain of Martello Towers, which was completed in 1810 just as the Napoleonic wars were coming to an end. Inside the Museum there is a surprisingly large area showing a wide range of artefacts and pictures depicting Seaford history plus fascinating collections of household and office equipment showing the development of everyday items. There are also tableaux of Victorian shops and homes with original objects in their appropriate settings.

The Museum is run entirely by volunteers of the Seaford Museum and Heritage Society and is a registered charity as well as being a registered museum. The Society also organises events each month in aid of Museum funds and they are regular social activities for the town. A virtual tour of the Museum is available on www.seafordmuseum.org

LITLINGTON
6 miles NW of Eastbourne off the A259

Dating back to Saxon times, this unspoilt village lies on the River Cuckmere and is best known for the **Litlington Tea House** which first opened over 100 years ago. Since then little has changed and visitors can still enjoy a full homemade afternoon tea in its relaxed and old fashioned atmosphere. The gardens around the tea house are equally enjoyable and sheltered from the road by ancient trees. During the summer the teas are served on the grassy terrace.

JEVINGTON
3½ miles NW of Eastbourne off the A22

This old smugglers' village was established during the time of Alfred the Great by another Saxon called Jeva. Inside the parish church is a primitive Saxon sculpture and the church tower dates from the 10TH century. During the 18TH century, when smuggling was rife in the area, the local gang brought their illegal goods up here from Birling Gap and stored them in the cellars of the village rectory. The gang's headquarters were the local inn and, conveniently, their leader was the innkeeper, a busy man who was also the ringleader of a group of highwaymen until he was hanged in the 1760s!

ALFRISTON
6 miles NW of Eastbourne off the A27

Alfriston is one of the oldest and best preserved (and consequently most popular) villages in Sussex. It is also convenient for the major holiday resorts. The settlement was founded in Saxon times and grew to become an important port on the River Cuckmere and a market town. The old market cross still stands in the square and is only one of two left in the county (the other is in Chichester).

One of the oldest buildings remaining in the town is the Star Inn, built in the early 15TH century as a resting place for pilgrims on their way to and from the shrine of St Richard at Chichester. Inside the original medieval carvings of animals on the ceiling beams can still be seen. Another ancient inn, the **Market Cross**, had no less than six staircases and acted as the headquarters of the notorious gang of smugglers led by Stanton Collins in the 19th century. Though he was never arrested for smuggling, Collins was eventually caught for sheep stealing, and as punishment (Though some might disagree!) was transported to Australia. It was tales of Collins and other local gangs which inspired Rudyard Kipling, living at nearby Rottingdean, to write his atmospheric poem, *A Smuggler's Song*.

YE OLDE SMUGGLERS INNE

Waterloo Square, Alfriston,
East Sussex BN26 5UE
Tel: 01323 870241

Situated in the picturesque village of Alfriston, **Ye Olde Smugglers Inne** is a beautiful black and white inn which dates back to 1358, and was once owned by a famous smuggler. The current landlady, Maureen Ney has a far more respectable background and has been running the pub since 1977. Inside, the olde world feel is continued with beams, old trinkets and an open fire, and there's also a pleasant conservatory area. Cooking is wholesome and uses premium quality local produce where possible.

SUSSEX OX

Milton Street, Alfriston, East Sussex BN26 5RL
Tel: 01323 870840 Fax: 01323 870715

Conveniently located for walkers near the start of
the South Downs Way, the **Sussex Ox** is overlooked
by Windover Hill and sits just a mile from the
historic centre of Alfriston. Called the Sussex Ox
as this was the last area in the county in which
oxen were used to pull farming machinery, this
well maintained inn serves refined pub fayre
cooked by Canadian chef Harry Findlay who is well
known in the locale for his culinary skills.

The former prosperity of this town is
reflected in its splendid 14TH century
parish church that is often referred to as
'the Cathedral of the Downs'. As
recently as the 1930s, local shepherds were
still buried here with a scrap of raw wool
in their hand - a custom which served to
inform the keeper of the gates of heaven
that the deceased's poor church
attendance was due to his obligation to his
flock!

Beside the church is the thatched and
timbered **Clergy House**, the first building
to be acquired by the National Trust for a
mere £10 in 1896. A marvellous example
of a 14TH century Wealden hall house, its
splendid condition today is due to the
skilful renovation of Alfred Powell who
managed to save both its crown pot roof
and the original timbers. Visitors to the

house can see an interesting exhibition
inside on medieval construction
techniques. The house is surrounded by a
magnificent and traditional cottage
garden that includes rare flowers that have
been grown since Roman times.

If it's time for a tipple, why not sample
some English wines at the **English Wine
Centre**. Housed in a charming, old
thatched roof building, the centre includes
a wine museum and a Time Garden which
incorporates many aspects of time through
its plantings and standing stones.

WILMINGTON
5 miles NW of Eastbourne off the A27

This delightful village, with its mix of
building styles, is home to the historic
remains of **Wilmington Priory**. Founded
in the 11TH century by William the
Conqueror's half brother,
Robert de Mortain, as an
outpost of the Benedictine
Abbey of Grestain in
Normandy, the priory was well
into decline by the time of the
Dissolution. Many of the
buildings were incorporated
into a farmhouse, but other
parts remain on their own
including the prior's chapel
which is now the parish
church of St Mary and St Peter.

However, the dominant
feature in Wilmington is its

Alfriston Market Cross

famous **Long Man**, that is cut into the chalk of Windover Hill and took its present form in 1874. There is much debate about the age of the Long Man and archaeologist and historians have been baffled for centuries. The earliest record of this giant is dated 1710 but this is inconclusive as it could be prehistoric or the work of an artistic monk from the local priory. However, what is known is that, at over 235 feet high, it is the largest such representation of a man in Europe. The giant, standing with a 250 foot long shaft in each hand, is, in many ways remarkable as, the design takes account of the slope of the hill and appears perfectly proportioned even when viewed from below. Covered up during World War II as the white chalk was thought to be a navigation aid to German bombers, it was outlined in concrete blocks in 1969.

Wilmington Long Man

ALCISTON
7½ miles NW of Eastbourne off the A27

This quiet hamlet, which once belonged to

ROSE COTTAGE INN

Rose Cottage Inn, Alciston, Near Polegate, Sussex, BN26 6UW
Tel: 01323 870377 Fax: 01323 871440

The **Rose Cottage Inn** is a perfect example of the quintessential English country pub. Set in the picturesque village of Alciston, just off the A27 and west of Polegate, the inn is tucked out of the way off the beaten track. Outside, its moss covered tiled roof and white weather boarded walls draped in climbing plants give way to an intimate, olde worlde interior. Beamed celings, open fires, boarded floors and walls create an enticingly cosy atmosphere. Owned by Ian and Ginny

Lewis, the pub has been in the Lewis family since 1959, and a pub since the turn of the 19th century.

The actual building, which was once two private dwellings dates back over 350 years. Food in the restaurant is top quality, using local produce as far as possible and featuring plenty of fresh fish and game when in season. Ginny has a talented catering team with customers coming back time and time again to sample their cooking, so much so that it is advisable to book ahead to avoid disappointment. Two locally brewed real ales are available year round, plus an old ale direct from the cask in Winter. A self catering flat with commanding views of the Downs is also available for rent.

Battle Abbey, became known as the "forgotten village" after its inhabitants fled following the ravages of the Black Death. Amongst other buildings, the villagers left a 13TH century church, which had been built on a hill on the foundations of a Saxon structure to avoid flooding, and 14TH century Alciston Court, that was once used by the monks.

Charleston Farmhouse

During the Middle Ages, the tenant farmers paid a rent to the abbot of Battle in the form of one tenth of their annual farm output, and at harvest time each year this was brought to the abbey's vast medieval tithe barn which can still be seen looming in front of the church. After the village was abandoned, Alciston Court became a farmhouse. The remains of a large medieval dovecote can also be seen close by. During the winter, large numbers of pigeons would be kept here to supplement the villagers' dreary winter diet.

SELMESTON
8 miles NW of Eastbourne off the A27

This ancient hamlet, which is sometimes misleadingly pronounced 'Simson', was the site where archaeologists discovered tools, weapons and pottery fragments in the churchyard during the 1930s which are thought to date from the New Stone Age. However, though the finds are interesting in themselves, Selmeston is better remembered as being the home of Vanessa Bell and her interesting domestic arrangements. Her house, **Charleston Farmhouse**, lies just west of the village and it was discovered by Vanessa's sister

and her husband, Virginia and Leonard Woolf, when she was looking for a country retreat for herself. Vanessa, an artist, moved here in 1916 with her art critic husband, Clive, and her lover, fellow artist Duncan Grant.

From then on and over the next 50 years, the house played host to the intellectual and artist group that became known as the Bloomsbury set and, for a time, both David Barnett and Maynard Keynes also joined the household. Other frequent visitors included Virginia and Leonard Woolf, who lived not far away at Rodmell, EM Forster and Roger Fry. During the 1930s, the interior of the house was completely transformed as the group used their artistic skills to cover almost every wall, floor, ceiling and even the furniture with their own murals, fabrics, carpet and wallpapers. They hung their own paintings on the walls, including a self portrait of Vanessa Bell and one of Grace Higgens, the valued housekeeper. The garden of the house too was not forgotten and a delightful walled cottage garden was created at the same time with carefully laid out mosaic pathways, tiled pools, sculptures and a scented rose garden. Following Duncan Grant's death

SILLETTS COTTAGE RESTAURANT

Church Farm, Selmeston, Near Polegate,
East Sussex, BN26 6TZ
Tel: 01323 811343 Fax: 01323 811743
e-mail:
enquiries@sillettscottage-restaurant.co.uk
website: www.sillettscottage-restaurant.co.uk

An unexpected and charming treat at Selmeston is **Silletts Cottage Restaurant**, a Grade II listed farmhouse, part of which dates back to the 16th century when it was originally built and named 'Church Farm' because its land was adjacent to the charming hamlet's church. The exact date when this fine building was constructed, 1540, is known because it has been carved onto one of the exposed beams up in the loft. Initially the building consisted simply of two downstairs front rooms, which have now been converted

into one attractive, open plan restaurant, open seven days a week for lunch and dinner and offering all the ingredients for a perfect meal in this idyllic country setting. Wonderful homecooked meals can be washed down with a fine bottle of wine from the approachable list in a quiet and laid back atmosphere, which is as appealing in summer as it is in winter.

During the summer months, guests can admire pleasant views of the Downs or soak up some sunshine sitting on the tasteful, wooden garden furniture scattered around the pretty, tree-encircled garden, and in the chilly winter months they can install themselves in front of the crackling log fire in the cocktail lounge. Owner Ron Sillett has two chefs, Neil Wakefield and Chris Butler who are in charge of the kitchen and prepare all of the food. They are both always open to new recipe suggestions, so visitors with any old favourite ideas tucked away at home should bring them along and show them to Ron. Despite being an imposing, ivy covered building from outside, Sillett's cottage is relatively small inside and its intimate restaurant can only seat a maximum of 40 to 50 diners.

The restaurant has a rustic feel, a collection of prints, brasses and other trinkets is spread over most available walls and beams, fresh cut flowers are placed on every table and potted plants are squeezed in from time to time adding a more modern touch. Lunch can be anything from a light snack to a substantial meal from the à la carte menu, and there's no minimum charge. Dinner can be chosen from a carefully compiled, fixed price selection with no hidden extra charges . Personal service is of the utmost importance to Ron and his devoted staff in this well-run establishment. They look after their guests superbly – nothing is too much trouble, and they genuinely want to know if there is anything they can do to make their visit more enjoyable. Visitors to Silletts Cottage are really left with no option but to enjoy their time here, and will no doubt be converted to the ranks of loyal fans who return again and again.

in 1978, a trust was formed to save the house and garden, restoring them to their former glory. This unique task has been described as 'one of the most difficult and imaginative feats of restoration' to be carried out in Britain. Attached to the house is a shop selected by the Craft's Council for the breadth and quality of its merchandise , which includes contemporary ceramics, a variety of cotton clothes and silk scarves, millinery, jewellery and furniture inspired by the Bloomsbury theme.

Just east of Charleston lies **St Michael and All Angels Church** in Berwick, which was decorated with murals painted by the Bloomsbury artists in the early 1940s.

UPPER DICKER
8 miles NW of Eastbourne off the A22

This hamlet, which overlooks the River Cuckmere, is centred around a minor crossroads in an area that was once known as 'Dyker Waste'. In 1229, Augustinian canons chose this as the site for the beautiful **Michelham Priory**. Founded by Gilbert de Aquila, the Norman Lord of Pevensey, the six acre site is surrounded on three sides by the River Cuckmere and on the other by a slow flowing moat - England's longest water filled medieval moat. The slow moving water is still used to power an old mill where traditionally ground flour is produced in small batches. A splendid gatehouse was added in the 14TH century and the priory continued to flourish until it was dissolved by Henry VIII in 1587.

After the Dissolution the priory came into the hands first of the Pelham family and then the Sackville family who, in the 300 years of their ownership, incorporated some of the priory's buildings into a Tudor farmhouse which went on to become the focal point of a large agricultural estate. Today, the grand Tudor farmhouse rooms are furnished with a collection of Dutch paintings, Flemish tapestries and old

THE LAMB INN
Church Lane, Ripe,
Near Lewes,
East Sussex BN8 6AS
Tel: 01323 811280

Built initially as farmworkers' cottages and once part of the Village Hall, **The Lamb Inn** is a charming old pub that dates back to the 18th century. A quintessential English country inn well recognised in the local community for its warm and familiar atmosphere and excellent food and drink selection, The Lamb is a freehouse run by Jill and Pete Baldwin since 2000. Both the chequered brick exterior and the cosy interior are very traditional, and stepping inside is like taking a step back in time. Wood abounds in the ceiling and in the wall panelling, and to make things even more inviting there are several open fires which blaze away when the North wind doth blow outside.

The bar and restaurant are made up of small alcoves which add to the intimate atmosphere. As well as its reputation for the high standard of freshly prepared, home cooked food using local produce whenever possible, The Lamb offers an impressive selection of cask ales on tap behind the bar, with Harveys available all year and two guest ales which are changed on a regular basis. There is also an exceptional wine list and broad range of beers and lagers from which to pick and choose.

SIX BELLS INN

Chiddingly, Near Lewes,
East Sussex BN8 6HE
Tel: 01825 872227

Built in the 1730s to revive weary stagecoach travellers, **The Six Bells Inn** still crouches right beside what was once a main thoroughfare - the busy London to Eastbourne road. Today however, this is a quiet and peaceful backwater, and husband and wife licensees Jacquie and Paul Newman offer their warm and friendly welcome mainly to long standing locals and walkers on the

nearby, popular Weald and Vanguard Ways. This attractive, old building with its low, tiled roof, chequered brick walls, white sash windows and low ceilings is almost cottage like in style and blends in totally with its neighbours in the village. During the summer, colourful hanging baskets bedeck the walls and bulging window boxes nestle under every window casting a rainbow of colours over the outside of the pub.

A popular and busy place throughout the year, The Six Bells has a cosy interior which is divided into several areas: the main bar with

its old, brick floor and exposed ceiling beams; the top bar which has an original Inglenook fireplace and a piano just in case of an impromptu sing a long; and the function room found at the top of a small, spiral staircase. The mass of local rugby team memorabilia, old posters and farming tools that cover the walls add to the convivial, village pub atmosphere. Thirsty customers can enter through the frosted glass door of the wooden porch and choose between the comfortable seating inside or the pleasant patio beer garden in which to quench their thirst.

Highly regarded for the range of real ales and stouts served behind the bar, The Six Bells is also gaining a reputation for its delicious homecooked menu that is served both at lunchtime and in the evening daily. Add to this the live music throughout the week and Jazz on Sunday lunchtimes and it is easy to see why so many people flock here. The pub has also attracted visitors of a less human kind over the years including the ghost of a grey cat and the spectre of Sara French who was hanged in Lewes in 1852 after being found guilty of poisoning her husband with arsenic in an onion pie. The jury for the trial, which became know as the Onion Pie Murder, sat in the top bar whilst deliberating their verdict.

English furniture and the gatehouse is home to a group of brass rubbings and a reconstructed forge.

Michelham Priory Gardens (see panel above) are equally interesting and they cover a range of styles. To the south of the house is a physic herb garden containing plants that were, and still are, grown for their medicinal and culinary benefits. There is also a recreated cloister garden which illustrates the ability of the original monks to combine a pleasing garden with one that requires little maintenance. There is also an Elizabethan barn in the grounds of the priory and a working watermill, and the river and moat attract a variety of waterfowl throughout the year.

MICHELHAM PRIORY

Upper Dicker, Hailsam, East Sussex BN27 3QS
Tel: 01323 844224 Fax: 01323 844030
e-mail: adminmich@sussexpast.co.uk

Michelham Priory boasts England's longest water filled medieval moat. Over a mile in length, it encircles nearly seven acres of beautiful grounds. on this picturesque island of history, you will find the impressive Gatehouse, a working watermill, and a magnificent (reputedly haunted) Tudor mansion that evolved from the former Augustinian Priory. With nearly 800 years of history, Michelham Priory offers visitors a wealth of interesting exhibits inside and out.

In the grounds ingenious planting of the landscaped gardens offers an ever-changing

display for the visitor whatever the season, from spring colour to a spectacular show of la summer herbaceous splenclour. The Physic Garden shows how our ancestors healed themselves. A recreated medieval cloister garden shows how the canons combined the practical and the pleasing with the minimum of maintenance.

Michelham Priory is situated at Upper Dicker, approx. 2 miles west of Hailsham and 8 miles north west of Eastbourne.

CHIDDINGLY
10½ miles NW of Eastbourne off the A22

This small village is dominated by the tall 15TH century spire of its church, which, at 130 feet is a useful local landmark. Inside the church is an impressive monument to Sir John Jefferay, Baron of the Exchequer under Queen Elizabeth, who lived at nearby Chiddingly Place - a once splendid Tudor mansion that has now been restored and sold as private accommodation. However,

his memorial is overshadowed by that of his daughter and son-in-law, who both appear to be standing on drums. Tradition has it that the Jefferay family once laid a line of cheeses from their manor house to the church door so that they would not get their feet wet. So the large discs of Sussex marble could, in fact, be a reference to those cheeses! Curiously, the monuments have lost hands and fingers over the years as enraged locals knocked them off thinking that the family were related to Judge Jefferies who presided at the Bloody Assizes.

LAUGHTON
11 miles NW of Eastbourne on the B2124

This scattered village, isolated on the Glynde Levels, was once home to

ROEBUCK INN

Lewes Road, Laughton, East Sussex BN8 6BG
Tel:01323 811464
e-mail: joyceroebuck@aol.com

Dating back in parts to the 14ᵗʰ century, **The Roebuck Inn** stands on the main street in the village of Laughton. This spacious, beamed free house serves an eclectic selection of beers and real ales, and accomplished home-made pub food, particularly the famous Roebuck pie. The Roebuck has also made quite a name for itself with its lively entertainment programme, which includes cabaret nights, candelit dinner dances, themed nights such as Bavarian, Cockney and Mowtown and licence to perform weddings.

flourishing marble mines, potteries and a brickworks. In fact, **Laughton Place** built in 1534 was one of the first brick buildings constructed in Sussex. The interior of the village church, which lies some way from the village centre, is dominated by a stone war memorial which features a soldier and sailor who have been carved in minute detail.

EAST HOATHLY
12 miles NW of Eastbourne off the A22

Situated some 20 miles from, West Hoathly, this compact village was immortalised by Thomas Turner in his *Diary of East Hoathly*. Although the village church was almost completely rebuilt in the mid 19TH century, the 15TH century squat tower remains from the original building. Known as a **Pelham Tower**, because it was built by the local Pelham family, the structure has a belt buckle carved on it on either side of the door. This distinctive emblem was awarded to Sir John Pelham for his part in capturing King John of France at Poitiers in 1356.

One of the door emblems has a deep slit in it that was supposedly caused by a bullet fired at Sir Nicholas Pelham in the 17TH century. The failed murderer is said to have been a Cavalier, Thomas Lunsford, who joined the French army after being exiled for attempted murder and returned to Britain to fight with the king during the Civil War before emigrating to America.

HALLAND
13 miles NW of Eastbourne on the A22

Just to the south of Halland lies the fascinating **Bentley House and Motor Museum**. Covering some 100 acres of beautiful Sussex countryside, the estate combines a wildfowl reserve, a stately home and a museum. Originally a modest 17TH century farmhouse, Bentley was transformed into the splendid Palladian mansion by the architect Raymond Erith who was also behind the restoration of 10, 11 and 12 Downing Street in the 1960s. Exquisitely furnished throughout, the house is particularly renowned for its Chinese Room and the Philip Rickman gallery which contains a collection of over 150 wildfowl watercolours by the celebrated Sussex artist.

The formal gardens surrounding the house are laid out in a series of rooms, separated by yew hedges, and they often follow a colour theme. Beyond are the grounds and a walk through the cool tranquility of Glyndebourne Wood.

Meanwhile, the renowned waterfowl collection, which includes swans, geese, ducks and flamingos and every kind of swan in the world, was begun in the 1960s by the late Gerald Askew and soon became the world's largest private collection . Free to roam in the glorious parkland, the emphasis at the wildfowl centre is on conservation and breeding, particularly of endangered birds.

5 The Cinque Ports and the East Sussex Coast

The story of this area of the East Sussex Coast is of course that of the events leading up to October 14, 1066. William, Duke of Normandy came here to claim the throne

of England and, after defeating Harold a few miles from the town of Hastings, this is exactly what he did. Hastings and Battle, the towns that grew up around the abbey that was built on the site of the battlefield, have a concentration of museums and exhibitions centred on the famous events of the 11TH century. The victorious Normans soon set about building castles and fortifications from which to

Hastings Town

defend their new territory and, along with the religious houses that they also founded, this area is rich in Norman architecture.

As the South Coast was susceptible to invasion in the days before the Royal Navy, the confederation of Cinque Ports was established to provide a fleet of ships able to defend it. Many of the towns that were part of the confederation seem unlikely sources of ships today because the silting up of many of the harbours has changed the

landscape of the East Sussex coast considerably in the last 1000 years. More recently, the coast has been the preserve of holiday makers taking advantage of a moderate climate and clean sea air. Popular spots include St Leonards that was created in the 1820s and went on to become a fashionable resort whilst the smaller and more modest Bexhill is home to the impressive modern De La Warr Pavilion that was constructed from steel in the 1930s.

Church Square, Rye

But Perhaps the most picturesque of the coastal towns here is the ancient town of Rye. Situated on a hill and once a great haunt for smugglers, Rye is a changing medieval centre.

THE CINQUE PORTS AND THE EAST SUSSEX COAST

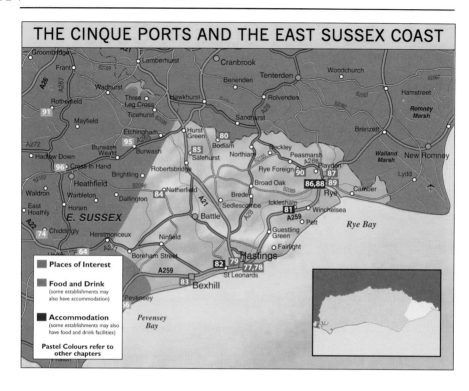

PLACES TO STAY, EAT, DRINK AND SHOP

HASTINGS

Long before William the Conqueror made his landing on the beaches of nearby Pevensey, Hastings was the principal town of a small Saxon province that straddled the county border between Sussex and Kent. Its name comes from 'Haestingas', a Saxon tribal name, and during the reign of Edward the Confessor, the town was well known for its sailors and ships. In fact, the town became so important that it even had its own mint. Earlier, during the 9th century when the Danes were occupying the town, the crowing of a cockerel, awoken by the movements of the townsfolk preparing to surprise their oppressors, alerted the occupying force to the uprising. And as a vengeance on all cockerels, the people of Hastings instituted a game called 'cock in the pot', where sticks were thrown at an earthenware pot containing a bird. Whoever threw the stick that broke the pot was given the cock as his prize and the game continued to be played each Shrove Tuesday until the 19th century. Mardi Gras is still a major celebration in Hastings and the Old Town Carnival is said to rival the festivities in the home of mardi gras, New Orleans.

Following the Battle of Hastings, which actually took place six miles away at Battle, the victorious William returned to Hastings where the Normans began to build their first stone castle in England. Choosing the high ground of West Hill as their site, they built **Hastings Castle**, which sadly is now in ruins and all that can be seen on the cliff top now are the original motte and parts of the curtain wall. However, there are commanding views from here and also the permanent 1066 Story display. Housed in a medieval siege tent, the exhibition, through clever use of audio-visual techniques, transports visitors back to October 1066.

West Hill also contains a system of elaborate underground passages, known as **St Clement's Cave**, where the naturally formed tunnel network has now been extended by man. The caves were leased to Joseph Golding, who spent a great deal of time fashioning the sandstone into sculptures, arcades and galleries and they became one of the town's first commercial sights and were used as air raid shelters during World War II. After the Conquest, this already important port became a leading Cinque Port, a role it played until the harbour was ruined in the Great Storm. Nevertheless, the fishing industry has managed to survive here and today fishing vessels continue to be hoisted on to the shingle beach by a winch. Indeed, this is the home of the largest beach-launched fishing fleet in Europe, and there's a fresh fish market too where you can stock up on the day's catch.

One of the town's most interesting features are the tall wooden huts that are used for drying nets and

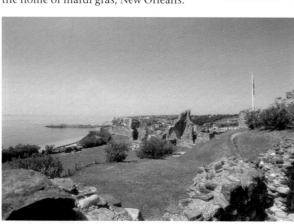

Hastings Castle

Hastings Beach

storing fishing tackle. Dating from the 17TH century, they are known as net shops or 'deezes'. The old fishermen's church of St Nicholas is now home to the **Fishermen's Museum**, which has as its centrepiece, *The Enterprise* - one of the last of Hastings' sailing luggers. Also here, amongst the displays of fishing tackle, model boats and historic pictures and

photographs, is *The Edward and Mary* - the first locally built boat to have an engine installed. Staying with a maritime theme, there is also the **Shipwreck Heritage Centre**, which is an award winning museum that is devoted to the history of wrecked ships. Exhibits on display here include a medieval sailing barge sunk on the River Thames in London, the warship, *Anne*, that was beached near Hastings in 1690, and *Primrose*, the last Rye barge. Additional displays show modern methods that help eliminate the possibility of a shipwreck, including radar and satellite navigation.

The old part of Hastings consists of a network of narrow streets and alleyways - or "twittens - which lie between West and East Hill. There are two cliff railways - one running up each of the hills. **West Hill**

YE OLDE PUMP HOUSE

64 George Street, Hastings Old Town, Sussex, TN34 3EE
Tel: 01424 422016

Tucked away down one of the many narrow side streets in Hastings Old Town, yet only yards from the seafront, **Ye Olde Pump House** was, as its name betrays, a former pump house. Built way back in the late 1400s, the building is crisscrossed with old wooden beams, both inside and out, and attracts patrons from all walks of life who soak up the atmosphere. Deep crimson upholstery contrasts with the dark wood in the pub's bar, whilst downstairs there is a wine/coffee bar. Food is simple and sensibly priced, with the emphasis on good quality ingredients. Upstairs is a charismatic en-suite room complete with a four poster bed, for those wishing to stay overnight.

THE STAG

All Saints Street, Hastings Old Town, Sussex, TN34 3BJ
Tel/Fax: 01424 425734
e-mail: info@thestag.org
website: www.thestag.org

Situated just yards away from the dockside, **The Stag** has built itself a solid reputation for serving a fine selection of seafood and for offering a varied and fun programme of live music. Housed in a smart, cream townhouse style building, it has a well thought out and inviting interior that would make anyone feel instantly at home. Not far from the pub is a self contained flat which can sleep up to six people.

Railway runs underground taking passengers to Hastings Castle and St Clement's Caves, whilst the East Hill Railway, the steepest in England, takes passengers to the cliff top and the beginning of **Hastings Country Park**. This 500 acre park is unlike the cliff tops around Eastbourne ,as the drop here is not sheer but is split by a series of sloping glens that are over hung with trees. The best way to discover the town's many interesting old residential buildings, inns and churches is to take a walk up the High Street and All Saints Street. **St Clement's Church**, in the High Street, has two cannonballs embedded in its tower, one of which was fired from a French warship, while the **Stag Inn** (see panel opposite), in All Saints Street, has a concealed entrance to a smugglers' secret passage as well as a pair of macabre 400 year old mummified cats!

Occupying the old Town Hall which was built in 1823, the **Museum of Local History** is an excellent place to come to for more information on this historic town. Going right back to the Stone Age, and with a considerable section on the Norman Conquest, the museum also covers Hastings' more recent past in displays on the rise of the Victorian resort, its life as a Napoleonic garrison and its role as a Cinque Port. The **Hastings Museum**

HASTINGS MARITIME STADE

c/o Stade Managers Office, Hastings Borough Council, 1st Floor, The Fishmarket, Rock-a-Nore Road, Hastings, Sussex, TN34 3DW
Tel: 01424 781377 Fax: 01424 781985
e-mail: tnewcomen@hastings.gov.uk
website: www.hastings.gov.uk

At the heart of the historic town of Hastings is the **Stade**, the shingle beach where the ancient Cinque Port meets the sea. Here is one of Britain's oldest and largest shore based fishing fleets, still using traditional wooden boats. Nearby wet fish shops sell fresh fish.The Net Shops are a series of black wooden huts standing in neat rows. Unique to Britain they were built to store fishing gear- with space at a premium they were built upwards like skyscrapers. A Fisherman's Museum in a former church contains a complete fishing boat. The 29 foot Enterprise is the last Hastings Lugger surviving in its original condition. Built on the Stade in 1912 it worked until 1955. The remains of a much older vessel can be found in the Shipwreck Heritage Centre. It's all that's left of a Roman ship. Also on display is the complete hull of a Victorian river barge and relics from a 1749 Dutch merchant ship whose wreck is visible at St Leonards at low tide. Both museums have free admission.

The sea creatures of the surrounding area can be seen at Underwater World where a dramatic glass tunnel under a huge tank allows visitors to walk under the ocean. Over 30 displays reveal all aspects of the lives of the local marine environment from shrimps to sharks. Built in 1902 the East Cliff Railway is one of the steepest in Britain and the journey to the top gives access to the Country Park and rewarding views of the Stade, Old Town and the coast.

and Art Gallery covers a wider range of exhibits including a dinosaur display which celebrates the fact that many fossils have been recovered near here, and also many of the county's ancient crafts. Hastings also contains a variety of attractions that are typical of a traditional seaside resort. The 600 foot long pier was completed in 1872 and had to be repaired after World War II when it was deliberately holed in two places to prevent it being used as a landing stage for Hitler's forces. According to local legend, the Conqueror's Stone at the head of the pier was used by William the Conqueror as a dining table for his first meal on English soil. The town also has its own version of the Bayeux Tapestry. Made by the Royal School of Needlework, the Hastings Embroidery comprises 27 panels that allow the viewer to walk through all the major events of the last 1000 years. Completed in 1966, among the many scenes and events depicted is the gentleman John Logie Baird - the Scottish pioneer of television who carried out many of his early experiments in Hastings.

Just outside of the town, the Marline Valley Nature Reserve is a steep sided, ancient woodland which supports a unique collection of plant and animal life and makes a beautiful setting for walking.

Old Cottages, Hastings

AROUND HASTINGS

BREDE
5 miles N of Hastings on the A28

Situated to the north of the River Brede, this compact village has a long history that is shrouded in myth and tales of the supernatural. One particular legend is that of the Brede Giant, based around the 16TH century owner of Brede Place, Sir Goddard Oxenbridge. At over seven feet tall he was certainly a giant and, by all accounts he was a God fearing gentleman of the parish. However, some time after his death stories spread that he was a child eating monster who was eventually killed by a band of Sussex children, who, having got him drunk, sawed him in half - the children of East Sussex holding down one end with the children of West Sussex securing the other!

BROAD OAK
7 miles N of Hastings on the A28

Tombs of the Oxenbridge family can be seen in the small Norman village church as can a wood carving of the Madonna created by Clare Sherida, - a cousin of Sir Winston Churchill who died aged 84 in 1970. A remarkable woman of her time, she travelled to America where she learnt to carve in wood whilst staying for six months on a Red Indian reservation. In the aftermath of the Russian revolution, she journeyed to Moscow and, stayed for two months at the Kremlin to carve busts of both Lenin and Trotsky.

NORTHIAM
9½ miles N of Hastings on the A28

This large and picturesque village is known for its characteristic white weather boarded cottages, some of which, along with a number of fine 17TH and 18TH century buildings, overlook the triangular green at the heart of Northiam. It was on this green that Elizabeth I is known to have dined and rested in 1573 under a great oak tree whilst on a journey through Kent and Sussex. Her green high heeled shoes must have been particularly uncomfortable as she took them off and left them to the villagers who saved them as a memento of her brief visit. Unfortunately, the vast oak tree, which was said to be over 1000 years old and was held together by chains and clamps, has died recently and all that remains now on the green is its giant stump.

Great Dixter House

Of the memorable buildings in the village, **Brickwall House** is one of the finest. This imposing 17TH century gentleman's residence was the home of the Frewen family, an old local family who had been living in Northiam since 1573 when the first Frewen came to the village as rector. Well known for its splendid plaster ceilings, there is also a comprehensive series of family portraits which begin in the 17TH century. On display in the house are also Elizabeth I's famous green shoes and a sedan chair that belonged to Martha Frewen, who burnt to death in her bedroom in the 1750s. Several members of the family were strict Puritans, and one father in particular who named his two sons, Accepted and Thankful. Despite the handicap of these unusual names, Accepted went on to become first the president of Magdalen College, Oxford and then the Archbishop of York, while Thankful is remembered for having donated the communion rails to the church in 1683. The church is also home to an impressive 19TH century family mausoleum. Brickwall House,

which is so named as the house and its grounds are surrounded by a high stone wall, also has some splendid topiary in the gardens, as well as an arboretum and a chess garden.

Just three miles northwest of Northiam lies **Great Dixter House and Gardens**, one of the finest examples of a late medieval house with the largest timber framed hall (which was moved here from nearby Benenden) in the country, surrounded by a very special garden. Built in the 1450s, the manor house was purchased in 1910 by Nathaniel Lloyd who then employed Edwin Lutyens to restore the house to its

Great Dixter Gardens

original medieval grandeur, as well as adding suitable domestic quarters for an Edwardian household, and the impressive Great Hall. Open to the public, many of the original rooms have been filled with antique furniture and examples of 18TH century needlework.

Kent and East Sussex Railway

However, it is the gardens that make Great Dixter so special. The imaginative design was laid out by Lutyens and, as well as including several existing outbuildings, various new features were added such as the sunken garden, the topiary lawn and the meadow garden. Begun by Nathaniel Lloyd and his wife Daisy, the gardens were added to by their son Christopher. A regular contributor on gardening to *Country Life*, Christopher's lively and inventive approach to horticulture obviously stems from working in the gardens. A mixture of formal and wild with many rare specimens, this is one of the most experimental gardens in the country.

Northiam is also the southern terminal for the **Kent and East Sussex Railway**, opened in 1900 it was the world's first ever full-size light railway, and was restored in 1990. There are now steam trains running on a track between here and Tenterden in Kent during the summer months. At one time too, the River Rother was navigable to this point and barges were brought upstream to be unloaded at the busy quay. This must have been an ancient port, as in the 1820s the remains of a Viking long ship were found in the mud by the river where they must have lain since the 9TH century.

Just north west of the town, the **Marline Valley Nature Reserve** is a steep sided, ancient woodland which supports a unique collection of plant and animal life.

BODIAM
10½ miles N of Hastings off the B2244

Situated in the valley of the River Rother, this attractive village, is home to one of the most romantic castles in the country. In the 1380s, Richard II granted Sir Edward Dalyngrygge a licence to fortify his manor house in order to defend the upper reaches of the then navigable River Rother. Thankfully, Dalyngrygge chose to interpret the licence in a very loose fashion and one of the last great medieval fortresses in England was built. Construction on **Bodiam Castle** was begun in 1385 when the technology of castle building was at its peak. Completely surrounded by a wide moat, the arrow slits, cannon ports and aptly named murder holes (through which objects were thrown at attackers below) were never actually used in anger. However, there was a minor skirmish here in 1484, and during the Civil War the castle surrendered without a shot being fired.

CASTLE INN

Main Street, Bodiam, East Sussex, TN32 5UB
Tel: 01580 830330 Fax: 01580 830040

Located right opposite the picturesque Bodiam castle, the **Castle Inn** is a spacious and traditional, red brick country inn. Inside the main bar, the beautifully hand-painted ceiling also depicts the historic castle. Wendy and James offer guests a warm welcome and a wide choice of home cooked food freshly prepared by James in the dining room overlooking the village green. There's also a large patio with picnic tables for open air dining when the weather is fine. Being a member of CAMRA, a large selection of traditional and seasonal ales are available. The nearby Kent and East Sussex steam railway makes a pleasant excursion.

A long period of decay followed, during the 17TH and 18TH centuries, until 1829 when plans to dismantle the castle were thwarted by 'Mad' Jack Fuller of Brightling. A programme of restoration was begun, firstly by George Cubitt at the end of the 19TH century, and completed by Lord Curzon in 1919. On his death in the 1920s, Lord Curzon left the castle to the National Trust and they have continued the restoration programme, including replacing the floors in the towers so that visitors can climb to the top of the battlements. Also a popular film location, as the exterior is almost complete and particularly romantic, while the interior remains somewhat bare.

PETT
4 miles NE of Hastings off the A259

Situated on top of a hill, the village overlooks **Pett Level** to the south - a vast

Bodiam Castle

Manor Farm Oast

Workhouse Lane, Icklesham, East Sussex TN36 4AJ
Tel/Fax: 01424 813787
e-mail: manor.farm.oast@lineone.net

Set in a traditional oast house, the **Manor Farm Oast** makes a refreshingly different place to stay. Built in 1860, the building exudes character with its two tall, conical towers and ruddy tiled roves and brick walls. Owned and run for the past five years by convivial hosts, Kate and Syd Mylrea, this award winning country retreat is situated in the middle of a working orchard and is ideal for a spot of walking in the surrounding countryside or retracing the path of some of the area's history with visits to Rye, Winchelsea, Battle or Hastings, which are all within easy striking distance.

expanse of drained marshland that now consists of watercourses and meadows. Dotted with small lakes the area provides a ideal sanctuary for wildfowl.

FAIRLIGHT
3 miles NE of Hastings off the A259

Separated from Hastings to the west by its country park, this village is a small settlement consisting mainly of old coastguard cottages. The 19TH century grey stone church occupies a magnificent position overlooking the coast and its tower can be seen for miles out to sea. So much so, that when the weathervane blew down the villagers were inundated with requests from anxious sailors asking for it to be replaced! In the churchyard, among a surprising number of elaborate tombstones, is the rather neglected final resting place of Richard D'Oyly Carte, the founder of the famous operatic company that will forever be linked with Gilbert and Sullivan.

To the west of the village lies **Fairlight Glen** - an attractive place where a gentle stream approaches the sea through a steep side woodland valley. The Lovers' Seat placed here is said to be in memory of a girl who waited on this spot for her lover to return to her from his ship. Unlike many similar tales, this one had a happy ending as, not only did the girl's lover return from overseas unharmed, but her parents also consented to their marriage.

ST LEONARDS
1 mile W of Hastings on the A259

St Leonards was created in the 1820s as a fashionable seaside resort by the celebrated

Melrose Guest House

18 De Cham Road, St Leonards on Sea, East Sussex, TN37 6JD
Tel: 01424 715163/422578 Fax: 01424 432772
e-mail: Melrose@fsmail.net

Sitting on the corner of a residential street in this traditional English seaside town, the **Melrose Guest House** is an imposing Victorian house. Built in 1888 and originally used as a college for the daughters of gentlemen, the house has been beautifully restored and transformed into a spacious B&B by current owners, Patricia and Roland Smith. The traditional English breakfast is aga cooked and served in the large, airy dining room with its original bay windows. Outside, there's a well-stocked garden and conservatory, and the beach is only a short 10 minute walk away.

London architect, James Burton, who was responsible for designing much of Bloomsbury. The centrepiece of Burton's plans was the Royal Victoria Hotel, which is now overshadowed by the vast **Marina Court** that was built to resemble an ocean going liner in the 1930s. Assisted by his son, Decimus, a talented architect in his own right who later designed the Wellington Arch at Hyde Park Corner in London, Burton went on to create a model seaside town that was designed to attract the wealthy and aristocratic.

De La Warr Pavilion

In the churchyard of the parish church, which was destroyed by a flying bomb in 1944 and rebuilt in a conservative modern style in the 1960s, lies Burton's curious tomb - a pyramid vault where he and several other family members are buried.

The delightfully informal **St Leonards Gardens** stand a little way back from the seafront and were originally private gardens maintained by subscriptions from the local residents. Acquired by the local council in 1880, they are now a tranquil area of lakes, mature trees and gently sloping lawns that can be enjoyed by everyone

BEXHILL
5 miles W of Hastings on the A259

This small seaside resort was founded in the 1900s by the influential De La Warr family who lived at the original village of Bexhill, just a mile from the coast. The old Bexhill was an ancient place, with its roots well established in Saxon times when the land around 'Bexlei' was granted to Bishop Oswald of Selsey by Offa, King of Mercia, in 772 and for a time it was also a haunt of

smugglers, before changing to the other side of the law and becoming a base for 6,000 Hanovarian troops of the King's German Legion from 1804 to 1814. Fortunately, a good many of the older buildings have survived the late 19TH century development including some old weather boarded cottages, a 14TH century manor house and the part Norman parish church.

Often referred to as Bexhill-on-Sea, this genteel resort was rather modest and doesn't have a pier although there is a promenade and some formal floral gardens. Among the many late Victorian buildings, the **De La Warr Pavilion** is the most impressive. Built in 1935 by Erich Mendelssohn and Serge Chermayeff, the De La Warr Pavilion is an impressive example of modernist architecture that was becoming fashionable at the time. Looking rather like an ocean going liner, with its welded steel frame, curves, abundance of glass and terraces, the Grade I listed building is now a renowned centre for arts and culture. With a 1000 seat theatre, which attracts many international artists, restaurant, bar and ball room, it is very much a focal point of the town. In the summertime, it is the place to go and enjoy some open air entertainment on its sheltered terraces.

For what would appear today to be a relatively conservative resort, Bexhill was the first seaside town to allow mixed bathing on it beaches in 1901! The gently sloping shingle beaches still offer safe and clean bathing. The town has another first: in 1902 it played host to the birth of British motor racing when a race and other speed trials were held here. The huge Edwardian cars - nine litres were not uncommon - almost flew along the unmade roads around Galley Hill, and stopping was a matter of applying the rear wheel brakes, brute force and luck! The anniversary of this first race is celebrated each year on the first Bank Holiday weekend in May with the Bexhill Festival of Motoring. For a fascinating journey through Bexhill's motor racing history, pay a visit to the **Motoring Heritage**

Centre at Sackville and the **Cooden Beach Heritage Gallery.**

Set in Manor Park with its romantic rose garden, the **Costume Museum** with its displays of toys, dolls and fashions from the mid 18th century is very enjoyable and a visit to the **Bexhill Museum** is worth while. As well as a range of exhibitions on local wildlife, history, geology and archaeology, there are also dinosaurs and even a Great Crab from Japan.

NINFIELD
7 miles NW of Hastings on the A269

To the north of this village, straggled along a ridge, lies Ashburnham Place - a red brick house that is sadly much less impressive than it once was. Now in private hands, the house was originally three storeys, but there have been many alterations over the years, including the addition of a new block in the 1960s. Meanwhile, the landscaped **Ashburnham Park**, has

BEXHILL-ON-SEA

Bexhill Tourist Information Centre

For town guide contact:
Tel: 01424 732208
e-mail: bexhilltic@rother.gov.uk

Set in the midst of 1066 country **Bexhill-on-Sea** offers a quiet charm and elegance, missing from many larger, better-known coastal towns. It's a great place to unwind and relax, walking along the two miles of straight promenade, studying the marine life in the rock pools or stopping for lunch at one of the many pavement cafes and restaurants. This was a favourite resort for the Victorians and modern visitors can still sit in the classic shelters they used, enjoying the same stunning views of Eastbourne, Beachy Head, Hastings and across the Channel. Bexhill has some of the finest Victorian and Edwardian buildings in England but it is the splendid De La Warr Pavilion that is its gem. This Art Deco delight was opened in 1935 and is one of the world's most sublime examples of modernist architecture. It has appeared in countless period films and televisions series including Agatha Christie's Poirot.

British Motor racing was born here in 1902 when Bexhill's seafront cycling boulevard became an international motor racing track. Amongst the 200 or so competitors in the very first races were such notables as H.S Rolls, of Rolls Royce, Baron Rothschild and Herbert Austin. Although racing ceased here when Brooklands Circuit opened there is still an annual celebration over the May Bank Holiday weekend. The three-day, Bexhill 100 International Festival of Motoring, where the car is the star, attracts some 80,000 visitors. More subdued but no less popular are the twice-yearly Anglo Continental Markets where the town centre is filled with stalls offering a genuine taste of France, Spain, Germany and Italy.

survived more or less on the grand scale in which it was conceived by Capability Brown in the 18TH century, though a large number of trees were lost in the hurricane of 1987.

Close to the house lies the parish church, where inside are several monuments to the landowning Ashburnham family. One member of the family, John Ashburnham, was a supporter of the monarchy in the Civil War and he followed Charles I on his last journey to the scaffold in London. Imprisoned in the Tower by Cromwell, the late king's possessions that he was wearing on the day of his death - his shirt, underclothes, watch and the sheet in which his body was wrapped - came into the hands of the Ashburnham family. These relics were kept in the church following the restoration of Charles II to the thrown and, for many years they were believed to offer a cure for scrofula, - a glandular disease called King's Evil - to anyone who touched them.

BATTLE
6 miles NW of Hastings on the A2100

This historic settlement is, of course, renowned as being the site of the momentous battle, on 14 October 1066, between the armies of Harold, Saxon King of England, and William, Duke of Normandy. The Battle of Hastings actually took place on a hill which the Normans called 'Senlac', meaning 'lake of blood', and even today some believe in the myth that blood seeps from the battlefield after heavy rain. However, any discolouration of the water is, in fact, due to iron oxide present in the subsoil. The battle was a particularly gruesome affair, even for those times, and it was not until late in the afternoon that Harold finally fell on the field - not from an arrow through the eye as is popularly believed, but from a series of heavy blows to the head and body. The myth that has grown up surrounding the manner of Harold's death can be traced back to a section of the Bayeux Tapestry where a spear can be seen passing behind Harold's head. However, the mystery of Harold's body remains just that. One story tells how it was buried by his mother at Waltham Abbey in Essex, while another suggests that William the Conqueror wrapped it in purple cloth and buried it on the cliff top at Hastings.

After the battle and subsequent victory, William set about fulfilling his vow that, if he was victorious, he would build an abbey. Choosing the very spot where Harold fell, **Battle Abbey** was begun straight away and was consecrated in 1094. Throughout the Middle Ages the Benedictine abbey grew increasingly wealthy and powerful as it extended its influence over wider and wider areas of East Sussex. This period of prosperity however came to an abrupt end in 1537

THE NETHERFIELD ARMS

Netherfield Road, Netherfield, Battle,
East Sussex TN33 9QD Tel: 01424 838282

The Netherfield Arms is a carefully maintained 17th century village inn with ornate bay windows and a white-clapboarded exterior which highlights the wonderful sea of hanging baskets and window boxes that covers the outside of the building. Set in a sleepy, little village, not far from Battle, the pub offers customers some delightful views as well as some very competent homecooked cuisine, which offers restaurant quality at pub prices.

Dormitory-under-Croft, Battle Abbey

The Prelude to Battle exhibition introduces visitors to the site and its history. This is followed by a video on the Battle of Hastings. Guides dressed in historical costume will lead you on a free interactive audio tour of the Battlefield, and you can also see the altar stone where Harold fell as you explore the atmospheric ruins. Other on-site attractions include an educational Discovery Centre and the recently rediscovered and consecrated Dunkirk Memorial, which was placed in the grounds in 1953 by the Men of the Trees organisation. Events are held on a regular basis.

There is also much more to Battle than the abbey and the battlefield and a stroll around the streets will reveal some interesting discoveries. The **Battle Museum of Local History** is an excellent place to learn more about the lives of those living in East Sussex through the ages and there is also a replica of the Bayeux Tapestry to view. Opposite the abbey, and housed in a 600 year old Wealden hall house, is **Buckleys Museum of Shops and Social History**, where more than 50,000 objects are displayed in authentic room settings which cover the period 1850 to 1950. There are also replicas of a Victorian kitchen, a 1930s country railway station and a bicycle shop.

when Henry VIII dissolved the monasteries. The abbey buildings were granted to Sir Anthony Browne, and during a banquet to celebrate his good fortune, a monk is said to have appeared before Sir Anthony announcing that his family would be killed off by fire and water. The prophecy was forgotten as the family flourished until some 200 years later in 1793, when the home of Sir Anthony's descendants, Cowdray Hall near Midhurst, burnt to the ground. A few days later another member of the family was drowned in the River Rhine in Germany.

Under the custodial care of English Heritage, Battle Abbey has much to offer the visitor.

Gate House, Battle Abbey

SEDLESCOMBE
6½ miles NW of Hastings on the B2244

This former flourishing iron founding settlement, is now a pleasant and pretty village, stretched out on a long sloping green, where the parish pump still stands under a stone building constructed in 1900. The interior of the church, on the northern edge of the village retains its seating plan of the mid 17TH century which clearly demonstrates the hierarchy of this rural society. The front pew was retained for the Sackville family with the other villagers seated behind. Right at the back, the last few pews were kept for 'Youths and Strangers'.

To the southeast of the village, centred around an adapted 19TH century country house, is the internationally renowned **Pestalozzi Children's Village**. Founded in 1959 to house children from Europe who had been displaced during World War II, the centre follows the theories of the Swiss educational reformer, Johann Heinrich Pestalozzi. This 19TH century Swiss gentlemen, who took orphans from the Napoleonic Wars into his care, believed that young people of all nationalities should learn together. The village now takes children from Third World countries who live here in houses under the care of a housemother of the same nationality. After studying for their first degree, the young adults return to their own countries where their newly learnt skills can be put to excellent use in the development of their homelands.

ROBERTSBRIDGE
10 miles NW of Hastings off the A21

Situated on a hillside overlooking the valley of the River Rother, the village's name is a corruption of *"Rothersbridge"*. In the 12TH century an annexe to a Cistercian Abbey was founded here by the river, and today some of the buildings can still be seen incorporated in a farm. The house's unusually high pitched roof protects the remains of the abbot's house, and in the garden there are other ruins. Robertsbridge has long been associated with cricket and, in particular, the manufacture of cricket bats. The village establishment of Grey Nicholls has made bats for many of the sport's famous names, including WG Grace, who stayed at The George Inn when visiting the village.

HURST GREEN
12 miles NW of Hastings of the A21

Set in four acres of gently sloping Weald farmland, close to the village, **Merriments Gardens**, is a place which never fails to appeal to its visitors. A naturalistic garden, where the deep borders are richly planted according to the prevailing conditions of the landscape, it has an abundance of rare plants. In contrast, there are also borders that are planted in the traditional manner of an English garden and are colour

SALEHURST HALT

Church Lane, Salehurst, Robertsbridge, East Sussex, TN32 5PH
Tel: 01580 880620

Sitting opposite a 12th century church, just outside the pretty village of Robertsbridge, **The Salehurst Halt** is a lovely Freehouse/Restaurant which dates back about 150 years. Inside, the pub has a warm and welcoming atmosphere and is filled with interesting furniture and bric-a-brac. Customers are able to enjoy a delightful country garden in the summer months and during the winter months there is an open log fire. Owners Colin and Sarah Green pride themselves on the variety and quality of their classic British cooking and efficient and friendly service.

themed using a mix of trees, shrubs, perennials and grasses. Things change at the gardens all the time, with the seasons, and as new ideas are put into operation.

RYE

This old and very picturesque town was originally granted to the Abbey of Fecamp in Normandy, in 1027, and was only reclaimed by Henry III in 1247. It became a member of the confederacy of the Cinque Ports, joining Hastings, Romney, Hythe, Dover and Sandwich as a key part of the south coast's maritime defence, and ascended to becoming a full Head Port in the 14TH century. Over the years, this hill top town which overlooks both the Rother estuary

Rye Town

and the Romney Marshes was subjected to many raids, including one by the French in 1377 which left no non stone buildings still standing. Later, the harbour suffered the same fate as many ports along the south coast as it silted up and it had to be moved further down the estuary. **Rye**

THE BENSON

15 East Street, Rye, East Sussex TN31 7JY
Tel: 01797 225131 Fax: 01797 225512

Set in the heart of the historic town of Rye, **The Benson** is a smart, three storey brick building. It started life as a home for a wealthy wool-merchant nearly three hundred years ago, before becoming a vicarage and then a hotel in 1976. Present owners, Peter and Valerie Sumner changed the name to Benson Hotel in honour of EF Benson (1867-1940), mayor of Rye and celebrated writer, whose characters included the now famous, Mapp and Lucia. The house is elegantly furnished, but its main appeal is as a base to explore the area.

Mid-week walking breaks are popular, and the Sumners provide maps and book guides if required. Rye lies at the heart of Romney Marsh – a haven for wildlife and a maze of walking paths. The cobbled streets and quiet winding passages of the town itself are crammed with history,

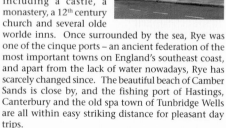

including a castle, a monastery, a 12th century church and several olde worlde inns. Once surrounded by the sea, Rye was one of the cinque ports – an ancient federation of the most important towns on England's southeast coast, and apart from the lack of water nowadays, Rye has scarcely changed since. The beautiful beach of Camber Sands is close by, and the fishing port of Hastings, Canterbury and the old spa town of Tunbridge Wells are all within easy striking distance for pleasant day trips.

Harbour Nature Reserve, on the mouth of the River Rother, is a large area of sea, saltmarsh, sand and shingle which supports a diverse range of both plant, animal and bird life.

Landgate, Rye

Rye's prominent hill top position was a factor which made it a strategically important town from early times. A substantial perimeter wall was built to defend the northern approaches and one of its four gateways, the imposing oak **Landgate,** still survives today and is all that remains of the fortifications erected by Edward III in the 1340s.

The town grew prosperous in the late medieval period due to the activities of its fishermen and the merchant fleets that traded with continental Europe. Though the loss of the harbour denied Rye its chief means of income and the town fell into decline, visitors today very much benefit from this turn of events as Rye has a large number of medieval buildings remaining which, with more money in the town, would have undoubtedly been demolished to make way for new structures.

Naturally, being a seafaring town, there is an abundance of old inns, and the **Mermaid Inn** - an early timbered building down a cobbled street is one of the most

famous. Rebuilt in 1420 after the devastating French raid over 40 years before, the inn was the headquarters of the notorious Hawkhurst Gang in the 18TH century - the most infamous band of smugglers on the south coast, in their day, who apparently always sat with their pistols close to hand in case of a sudden raid by the excisemen.

Another interesting building is the handsome Georgian residence **Lamb House,** which is now in the hands of the National Trust. Built by a local wine merchant, James Lamb in 1723, the house was home to a well known and influential family in the town. Not long after the house was built in 1743, the family was involved in Rye's famous murder, when a local butcher named Breads killed James

THE QUEENS HEAD

Landgate, Rye, East Sussex TN31 7LH
Tel: 01797 222181

Dating back to the 17th century, **The Queens Head** is situated in the bustling town centre of Rye. Its black and white exterior which has changed little since it was built, blends in perfectly with the rest of this historic town. Simple snacks are available in the bar, or there's a more diverse choice on the à la carte menu in the restaurant, focusing on fresh, local produce. For a longer stay, there are five comfortable rooms available upstairs.

Lamb's brother-in-law by mistake. His intention had been to murder James, Rye's Lord Mayor, with whom he held a grudge. Tried and found guilty, Breads was hanged on a gibbet and his bones were then stolen to be used as a cure for rheumatism. Only his skull survives and it can still be seen, along with the gibbet, in Rye Town Hall.

More recently, Lamb House, was the home of the novelist, Henry James, who lived there from 1898 to 1916 and many of his personal possessions are on show in the house. James was also responsible for laying out the gardens and he invited many of his friends to the house, including HG Wells, Rudyard Kipling, CK Chesterton and Joseph Conrad. The literary associations do not end there as in

Mermaid Street, Rye

the 1920s, the property was leased to EF Benson who is best remembered for his Mapp and Lucia books which include descriptions of the town that he thinly disguised as 'Tilling'.

Rye's oldest surviving buildings is **Ypres Tower** built in 1249, which forms part of

OLD BOROUGH ARMS HOTEL

The Strand, Rye, East Sussex TN31 7DB
Tel/Fax: 01797 222128
e-mail: info@oldborougharms.co.uk
website: www.oldborougharms.co.uk

Up a flight of ivy covered steps at the foot of Rye's famous Mermaid Street, the white clapboard façade and striking blue shutters of the **Old Borough Arms** hotel make a welcome sight to any weary traveller. This very pleasant guest house offers excellent accommodation in a 300 year old former smugglers' inn, incorporating part of the 14th century town wall, constructed to protect Rye from French invaders. A warm welcome into this cosy, family run establishment is extended by owners Lynn and Glynne Norris, who have made sure that this is a real home from home. Their aim is to make sure all guests have a relaxing and enjoyable stay in Rye.

Breakfast is served in the oak panelled breakfast room on the first floor overlooking the morning's comings and goings on The Strand down below and includes full English, vegetarian and many other permutations such as kippers. Fresh, local produce is always used when it's available. The flower bedecked patio provides another vantage point for people watching in Rye's bustling Strand, full of interesting antique shops; the harbour is nearby. The hotel's nine bedrooms are all ensuite. Two are spacious family rooms, and two are home to luxurious four poster beds. Booking is recommended, as this is a popular place. The hotel has a non smoking policy.

RYE CASTLE MUSEUM

Ypres Tower, 3 East Street,
Rye, East Sussex TN31 7JY
Tel: 01797 226728

Rye Castle Museum is the local museum for Rye and is on two sites: one is a medieval tower, built in 1249, and is the oldest building in Rye open to the public; the second is in East Street and it tells the story of Rye's illustrious past. East Street exhibits Rye's c18th fire engine, the famous pottery made in Rye, toys, maritime objects from Rye's shipbuilding past, and much more from Rye life over the last two hundred years. The Tower has changing displays and from its balcony is a magnificent view of what was once Rye's harbour and is now the Romney Marsh.

the **Rye Castle Museum** - the other part being in East Street (see panel below). The collection concentrates on the town's varied past and includes exhibitions on smuggling, law and order and the story of Romney Marsh sheep. Meanwhile on the second site, there is an old fire engine, pottery made in the town, nautical equipment and much more. Combining the traditional craft of model making with the latest electronic techniques, the **Rye Heritage Centre** presents a model of the town, complete with light and sound, that transports visitors back through the ages.

Rye Art Galleries house a permanent collection which focuses on 20th century British art, and also a changing programme of exhibitions featuring local

artists. For something very unusual, try the **Mechanical Music Exhibition** at Rye Treasury, which has an amazing collection including barrel organs, hand-cranked reed organettes and a 1920s Mortier Dance Organ.

If you happen to be visiting Rye in September, make sure you take in the acclaimed Rye Festival of Music and the Arts.

AROUND RYE

PLAYDEN
1 mile N of Rye off the A268

This smart hamlet has a rather battered old 12TH century church, with a shingle broach spire, that houses an unusual memorial to a 16TH century Flemish brewer. A refugee from Spanish persecution in the Low Countries, Cornelis Roetmans settled in the area along with a community of Huguenots. He carried on

RUMPLES INN

Peasmarsh Road, Rye Foreign, Rye, East Sussex, TN31 7SY
Tel/Fax: 01797 230494
e-mail: Gloria@borntocook.freeserve.co.uk
website: www.rumplesinn.co.uk

A spacious, white panelled roadside establishment, the **Rumples Inn** combines a traditional pub with a restaurant and motel style accommodation. Located just far enough outside of Rye to have a rural appeal, the site is large and includes ample outdoor seating. Run by a husband and wife team, the inn serves an extensive range of the best of French, English and Thai cuisine, which is often accompanied by some live music.

his trade as a brewer and, after his death, he was remembered in the church by a memorial slab that is carved with beer barrels and mash forks - the tools of his trade!

The country lanes to the northeast of Playden lead to the start of the **Royal Military Canal**, an unusual waterway that was built in 1804 as part of the defences against a possible invasion by Napoleon. There is a 20 mile long towpath between Rye and Hythe which offers easy and attractive walking along the fringes of the now drained Walland and **Romney Marshes**.

CAMBER
3 miles SE of Rye off the A259

The village has seen a lot of development since World War II with the building of bungalows on the sand dunes. However, despite its relatively modern appearance, Camber is also home to **Camber Castle** - a fine example of a series of coastal defences built by Henry VIII in the 16TH century. Now in the hands of English Heritage, the fortress seems surprisingly far inland today (due to the receding tides) though when it was built, it held a commanding position on a spit of land on one side of the Rother estuary.

WINCHELSEA
2½ miles SW of Rye on the A259

Though Winchelsea lies only a short distance from Rye, there could be no greater contrast: whilst Rye is a hive of tourist bustle, Winchelsea is a quiet place that time seems to have forgotten. An ancient Cinque Port and the smallest town in England, Winchelsea lay several miles to the south in the 13th century on a site which was eventually engulfed by the sea after a series of violent storms.

The 'new' Winchelsea stands on a hill and was built to a rigid grid pattern laid out by Edward I. The ambitious rectangular plan of 39 squares - a feature which can still be seen some 700 years later - became the home of around 6000 inhabitants which is nearly 10 times the number of residents today!

For a short time in the 14TH century Winchelsea prospered as the most important Channel port, but again nature took its toll and the town lost its harbour. The port went into decline and, along with the Black Death and constant raids by the French, the town fell into almost complete obscurity. It was not until the mid 19TH century that a successful recovery plan was put together to restore the town to something like its former grandeur and historic beauty. **Winchelsea Court Hall Museum** illustrates the events that led to the town's prosperity culminating in it being made a Head Port of the confederation of Cinque Ports, and then to its gradual decline. The museum is housed in one of Winchelsea's oldest surviving buildings, and close by can be seen the ruins of a 14TH century **Franciscan Friary**.

Today, Winchelsea has a particular charm that has attracted artists and writers here throughout the 20TH century.

BECKLEY
4½ miles NW of Rye on the B2088

When Alfred the Great died in 900, he referred to lands at 'Beccanleah' in his will and there was certainly a Saxon church here though a more modern building stands on the site today. Inside the medieval building which has a Norman tower, are two grotesque stone heads with leaves protruding from the mouths that were known as 'jack in the greens'. On still nights, it is said that Sir Reginald Fitzurse can still be heard riding furiously to the church for sanctuary after taking part in the murder of Thomas à Becket!

6 Ashdown Forest and the Sussex Weald

This region of East Sussex, centred around the ancient Ashdown Forest - a royal hunting ground that also provided the fuel for the area's iron industry - is characterised by small towns and villages of beamed cottages, traditional hall houses and farms. Inevitably, much of the actual woodland has been lost both as fuel and for shipbuilding. Though the area has been inhabited from ancient times, the discovery of a supposedly 150,000 year old skull in 1912 at the village of Piltdown caused much excitement before it proved to be a hoax some 40 years later!

Over the centuries there have been many fine houses and castles constructed in the area and, in particular, there is the impressive Herstmonceux Castle. Home of the Royal Observatory from 1948 until the 1980s, this magnificent medieval brick fortress, which also provided comfortable living accommodation for its inhabitants, is also set in beautiful gardens and parkland.

Other houses in the area have a more personal appeal and one, Bateman's at Burwash, was the home of Rudyard Kipling from 1902 until his death in 1936. A quiet place in a secluded position, the house has been left as it was when Kipling died and is full of his personal possessions. Ashdown Forest and Hartfield are also linked with another 20TH century novelist - AA Milne. He lived close by and set his Winnie the Pooh stories that he wrote for his son Christopher Robin in the forest and surrounding area.

Sheffield Park Gardens

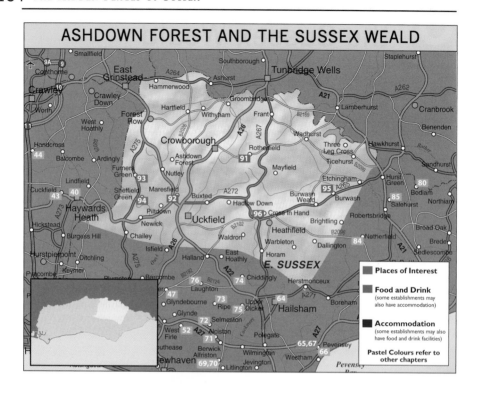

ASHDOWN FOREST AND THE SUSSEX WEALD

PLACES TO STAY, EAT, DRINK AND SHOP

CROWBOROUGH

This Wealden town on the eastern edge of Ashdown Forest is, at over 750 feet above sea level, one of the highest towns in Sussex. Before the arrival of the railways in the 1860s, this was a small community of iron smelters and brigands centred around the parish church and vicarage which dates from the 18TH century. However, the railways put Crowborough within easy reach of London and it was gradually transformed into a flourishing town.

On the highest place in Crowborough stands **Beacon House** built in 1838 and one of the town's oldest buildings. At the heart of the town is a triangular green, where another building stands - the grey stone classical church which dates from

1744. Its convenient location meant that the town attracted a number of well known late 19TH century writers, in particular Sir Arthur Conan Doyle, creator of Sherlock Holmes.

AROUND CROWBOROUGH

GROOMBRIDGE
4 miles N of Crowborough on the B2110

This unspoilt village straddles the county border with Kent, and although the Sussex part of the village which grew up around the railway station has little to offer, the Kent side is particularly charming. Centred around a triangular green are attractive 15TH and 16TH century estate

THE CATTS INN

High Street, Rotherfield,
East Sussex TN6 3LH
Tel: 01892 852546

Sitting by the roadside in the centre of Rotherfield, and looking from the outside very much like a private residence with neat net curtains hanging at the windows, is **The Catt's Inn**. Built in the 16th century, it was originally an alehouse, then it later became an inn named after local residents, the Catt family who were once Lords of the Manor. This traditional village hostelry is a freehouse, knowledgably owned and managed by Fred and Monica Jones who have been landlords here since 1990, having previously been the driving force behind the Royal British Legion at Horsted Keynes.

Together with the help of their daughter Derby and the latest family member, Buster the terrier, they give all their customers a personal and friendly welcome. Fred is the galloping gourmet who rules the roost in the kitchen, conjuring up an exciting daily selection of meals and snacks. All Fred's delicious dishes are cooked fresh to order and even the chips are home-made! The cooking is complimented by a sizeable range of traditional real ales and lagers. Being a lively establishment, the Catts Inn is a firm favourite with locals, but the Jones family also ensures that visitors are made to feel more than welcome. Most nights there is entertainment of some sort or other in the bar, from crib and darts tournaments to pub quizzes, and at the weekends football is the name of the game. Much of these activities benefit charities and local good causes, so you may well be asked to dig deep and donate to the latest appeal when you drop by.

cottages and a superb manor house, **Groombridge Place** which dates from the 17TH century. However, the site on which the foundations were laid is much older and there is some evidence that there was initially a Saxon and then a Norman castle here. Built by Charles Packer, the Clerk of the Privy Seal who accompanied Charles I on his unsuccessful journey to Spain to ask for the Infanta's hand in marriage, it is a splendid red brick house surrounded by a moat and set within beautiful terraced gardens (which are occasionally open to the public), and woodland that has been dubbed the Enchanted Forest. Being a staunch Protestant, Charles Packer also had the chapel built in thanks that the king's mission to Spain failed.

HADLOW DOWN
4 miles SE of Crowborough on the A272

This handsome hamlet is surrounded by undulating lanes that weave their way through some of the most glorious Wealden countryside. Just outside Hadlow Down is the **Wilderness Wood** - a unique family run woodland that does much to maintain the crafts and techniques of woodland management. Visitors can see the area being tended as they wander through the traditional chestnut coppices and plantations of pine, beech and fir. The wood is then harvested and the timber fashioned using traditional techniques into all manner of implements in the centre's workshops. This is very much a living museum of woodland management. There are also woodland trails, a pretty bluebell walk in spring.

WALDRON
7 miles S of Crowborough off the B2192

The 13TH century village church of All Saints has a lovely kingpost roof and, unusually for its age, a very wide aisle and nave, the reason for which has never quite been explained.

BUXTED
5 miles SW of Crowborough on the A272

The history of this village has been dominated by the still privately owned house, **Buxted Park**. The present house that was nearly destroyed by fire in 1940, was built along classical lines in 1725, but was greatly altered by architect Basil Ionides and various items, including the main staircase and front door, actually came from other buildings. In the 19TH century the house was the home of Lord Liverpool, who wishing to give himself more privacy, decided to move the entire village further away! The villagers were incensed and refused to move, so reaching a stalemate, Lord Liverpool declined to repair their estate cottages.

Eventually, the villagers gave way and moved to the village that is now Buxted. However, several buildings have remained in the old location including the half timbered **Hogge House** by the entrance to the park gates. Dating back to the 16TH century, the house was once the home of Ralph Hogge who is said to have been the first man to cast guns in England in 1543. The much restored 13TH century parish church also remains in the park's grounds and the Jacobean pulpit was once used by William Wordsworth's brother who was vicar here for a time.

MARESFIELD
5½ miles SW of Crowborough off the A22

Before the turnpikes between London and the south coast were laid through the Weald this was a remote place, but the 18TH century saw the development of Maresfield due to its location at a crossroads. The tall Georgian Chequers Inn is arguably the village's oldest building and a fine example of a coaching inn. Close by is a white painted iron milestone with the figure 41 and four bells and bows in outline. One of a whole chain of such

THE CHEQUERS INN

Maresfield, Nr Uckfield, East Sussex TW22 2EH
Tel: 01825 763843 Fax: 01825 767504

Housed in an elegant, period style mansion building, and located
in an area regarded as one of the most sought after addresses in
Sussex, **The Chequers Inn** comprises 17 luxury rooms, a
charming restaurant serving top quality, modern English cuisine
and a cosy, classically decorated bar. Landlord Keith Western
prides himself on his exceptionally high standards and on his
food, which is why The Chequers is regularly full with satisfied
diners savouring the globally inspired menu, with its strong emphasis on seafood and fish. Dark oak
walls combined with a large stand in fire place makes this a particularly cost retreat on wintry days.

milestones that stood on the old turnpike
road, this is a particularly witty one as it
refers to the distance in miles from
Maresfield to the Bow Bells in London.

PILTDOWN
7½ miles SW of Crowborough off the A272

Although this village is not generally well
known, it is famous in academic circles. In
1912, an ancient skull was discovered by
the Lewes solicitor and amateur
archaeologist, Charles Dawson in the
grounds of Barcombe Manor. At the time,
archaeologists the world over were looking
for a 'missing link' between man and the
ape and the skull seemed to fit the bill - it
had a human braincase and an ape like
jaw. Believed to be about 150,000 years
old it was not until the 1950s, and with
much improved scientific dating
techniques, that the skull was proved to be
a fake. It was in fact, the braincase of a
medieval man who had suffered a bone

thickening disease and the jaw of an
orangutan. The perpetrator of the hoax
was never discovered. It certainly could
have been Dawson himself, but various
other theories have been put forward
including one which points to Sir Arthur
Conan Doyle, the author of the Sherlock
Holmes stories and a well known Christian
fundamentalist...

Though the skull has been proved a
hoax, the village inn, which changed its
name to the **Piltdown Man** in 1912, still
carries the name and an inn sign with the
famous skull on one side and a stone
carrying humanoid on the other.

UCKFIELD
7 miles SW of Crowborough on the B2102

Situated in the woodland of the Weald on
the River Uck, this was once a small village
at the intersection of the London to
Brighton turnpike road with an ancient
pilgrims' way between Canterbury and

HEAVEN FARM

Furners Green, Uckfield, Sussex TN22 3RG
Tel: 01825 790226 Fax: 01825 790881
e-mail: Butler.Enterprises@farmline.com
website: www.heavenfarm.co.uk

Heaven Farm is a charming, family run leisure business
set in parkland and found in the heart of the Sussex Weald.
Take a tour around the cluster of old farm buildings, now
a museum, to see how things were done when built back
in 1830, or walk our popular and unique nature trail with
Wallabies, ponds, woods and Greenwich Meridian etc. The
site also contains a gift shop (picture), stable tea rooms (coffee, light lunches, cream teas), and a caravan
and camp site. Open March-October 10am-5pm.

The National Trust

THE NATIONAL TRUST SHEFFIELD PARK GARDEN

Sheffield Park, East Sussex, TN22 3QX
Tel: 01825 790231 e-mail: sheffieldpark@nltrust.org.uk
Fax: 01825 791264 website: www.nationaltrust.org.uk

This is a magnificent landscaped garden, laid out in the 18th century by 'Capability' Brown and further developed in the early years of the 20th century by its owner, Arthur G. Soames. The centre piece is the original series of four lakes. There are dramatic shows of daffodils and bluebells in spring, and the rhododendrons, azaleas and stream garden are spectacular in early summer. Autumn brings stunning colours from the many rare trees and shrubs. The short walk towards the neo-Gothic Sheffield Park House is bordered by several autumn foliage trees and shrubs including maples, photinias, nyssas and fothergillas.

Even in winter there are spectacular views and many splendid walks, the most spectacular of which, is the Big Tree Walk with its fine specimens of North American Sequoia. The walk goes past oak and beech under planted with hardy hybrid rhododendrons and towards the end of the first lake is a superb specimen of the rare, Mexican Pinus Montezumae planted in 1910.

At the head of the first and second lakes is a fine specimen of Blue Cedar. The banks of those lakes are broken by rounded clumps of pink, white and crimson rhododendrons. Just past the first bridge the main path goes through groups of deciduous and evergreen azaleas and some fine old lime trees. Beyond the lower bridge is a fine view of a magnificent waterfall and in summer the lake is covered with deep pink and white flowered water lilies. The path continues to a large Copper Beech and a Cedrus Atlantica, where superb views across the first lake take in a landscape full of silver birch, oaks and conifers.

An extended tour of the gardens should include the Aucklandii Walk with its Hydrangea ' Blue Wave', a small specimen of Eucalyptus Gunnii, some wonderful Rhododendron 'Angelo' and several large groups of pink Japanese azaleas. The Conifer Walk although devastated by the storm of 1987 contains many young specimens propagated from the original trees as well as a fine Acer saccharinum. The Gentian Walk, with its two long beds of blue Chinese gentian, leads into the Stream Garden and the Seven Sisters Glade. The former is at its best in the late spring and early summer when its plantings of hostas, astilbes, ferns, Siberian iris, lilies and Asiatic primulas are at their peak. The Giant Lily of the Himalayas is undoubtedly the top attraction here with its large scented white flowers on stems at least eight feet high. Beyond the Glade, replanted after the storm, is a grove of, superb, autumn-coloured, Tupelo trees that have already reached sixty feet in height.

On the bank of the fourth lake two fine specimens of Dawn Redwood and Swamp Cypress stand in front of clumps of the huge Brazilian Gunnera with its six-foot wide leaves. The Cascade Bridge, which crosses the cascade between the third and four lakes is haunted, according to legend, by a headless woman, who vanishes when approached.

Winchester. Before the stage coaches arrived and a number of coaching inns sprang up, Uckfield, due to its position close to woods and water, was a centre of the iron industry. However, despite these advantages Uckfield remained small until the 19TH century, when a period of rapid expansion inevitably followed the arrival of the railway.

Several of the old coaching inns survived the move from horsedrawn to steam powered travel, and amongst the Victorian buildings, **Bridge Cottage** is a fine example of a medieval hall house.

SHEFFIELD GREEN
8 miles SW of Crowborough on the A275

The village takes its name from the manor house - a Tudor building that was remodelled in the 1770s by James Wyatt for John Baker Holroyd MP, the 1ST Earl of Sheffield. At the same time as creating his mansion, **Sheffield Park** (see panel opposite), the earl commissioned Capability Brown to landscape the gardens. During the last months of his life, Edward Gibbon the earl's great friend came to stay and whilst here wrote much of his epic *Decline and Fall of the Roman Empire* in the library.

The 3RD Earl of Sheffield, a later inhabitant, was a keen cricketer and initiated the test tours between England and Australia. At the same time he began a tradition, which lasted until just a short while ago, that the visiting team came to Sheffield Park to play their first match against the Earl of Sheffield's XI. Though the house remains in private hands, the splendid Gardens owned by the National Trust are open to the public.

Not far from the house in the village, lies the Sheffield Arms, a coaching inn that was built by the 1ST Earl in the 18TH century. Local stories spoke of a cave

behind the inn with an underground passageway to a nearby farmhouse that was used by smugglers, so to test out the truth of the tales, three ducks were shut into the cave, and after ten days one of the ducks reappeared in the cellars of the farmhouse!

The village is also the terminus of the **Bluebell Railway,** and the cricketing earl would have been pleased with the railway's success today as he was on the board of the Lewes and East Grinstead Railway that originally built the line. The other terminus can be found near East Grinstead.

CHAILEY
9 miles SW of Crowborough on the A275

This large and scattered parish comprises three villages: North Chailey, Chailey and South Common. Though small, Chailey has some impressive old buildings including the 13TH century parish church and a moated rectory. To the north lies **Chailey Common** - a nature reserve covering some 450 acres of wet and dry heathland where Chailey Windmill is also located. Unlike many Sussex windmills, Chailey's splendid smock mill was saved from ruin just in the nick of time.

Overlooking the common is **Chailey Heritage**, which was founded in 1903 as a home for boys with tuberculosis from the East End of London. As treatments for the now less prevalent disease have progressed, the home has become a learning centre for children with disabilities and has a world wide reputation.

NUTLEY
5 miles SW of Crowborough on the A22

The village is home to **Nutley Windmill,** Sussex's oldest working windmill, which was restored in 1968 by a group of enthusiasts after it had stood unused and neglected from the turn of the century.

ASHDOWN FOREST
3 miles W of Crowborough on the B2026

This ancient tract of sandy heathland and woodland on the high ridges of the Weald is the largest area of land never to have been ploughed and put to agricultural use in south east England. The original meaning of 'forest' was as a royal hunting ground, and this is exactly what Ashdown Forest was. The earliest records date from 1268 and its thriving population of deer made it a particular favourite sporting place. However, the area was used long before this, and in prehistoric times there was a network of trackways across the forest. Later, the Romans built a road straight across it and by the time of the Norman invasion, the rights of the commoners living on its fringes to gather wood for fuel, cut peat and graze cattle, were well established.

During medieval times it was a great place for sport and a 'pale' or ditch was dug around it to maintain the deer within its confines. It was during the ownership of one famous sporting owner John of Gaunt, the Duke of Lancaster that the forest became known as Lancaster Great Park. Henry VIII and James I were also frequent visitors. However, by the end of the 15TH century much of the woodland had gone, used as fuel for the area's iron industry, and during the chaos of the Civil War the forest was neglected and by 1657 no deer remained.

Today, the deer have returned and the forest is a place of recreation with many picnic areas and scenic viewpoints.

HAMMERWOOD
7 miles NW of Crowborough off the A264

Here, down a potholed lane, is **Hammerwood Park** - a splendid mansion built in 1792 by Benjamin Latrobe, the architect of the Capitol and the White House in Washington DC. Set within romantic parkland, the house has had a chequered time over the years, including being the home of a member of the rock group Led Zeppelin in the 1970s and being rescued from ruin in the 1980s. Restoration work has been undertaken by the present owner and whilst there are some massive murals in the hall, the dining room has been left derelict. The house is open on a limited basis during the summer.

HARTFIELD
4 miles NW of Crowborough on the B2026

An old hunting settlement on the edge of the Ashdown Forest, which takes its name from the adult male red deer or hart, the village is very closely associated with AA Milne and Winnie the Pooh. Milne lived at Cotchford Farm, just outside Hartfield and he set his famous books which he wrote in the 1920s, in the forest. Designed to entertain his son Christopher Robin, the books have been delighting children ever since, and with the help of illustrations by EH Shepard, the landscape around Hartfield has been brought to millions around the world.

In the village lies the 300 year old sweet shop where Christopher Robin was taken each week by his nanny. Now called **Pooh Corner**, this is a special place to visit for both children and those who remember the stories from their own childhood as it has the largest selection of Pooh memorabilia in the world. All of the places in the books lie within the parish of Hartfield, including **Poohsticks Bridge** - a timber bridge spanning a small tributary of the River Medway – which was restored in 1979.

WITHYHAM
3½ miles NW of Crowborough on the B2110

This small village with its church and pub was also the home of the Sackville family from around 1200. In 1663 the original village church was struck by lightning that was said to have come in through the steeple, melted the bells and left through the chancel, tearing apart monuments on its route. The view from the front of the rebuilt church, over a stretch of grass and across fields to Hartfield in the distance, is a view that hasn't changed in hundreds of years.

Inside the church is a large mural painted by an Earl De La Warr who was

Bateman's

rector here in the 19TH century (the De La Warr family was a branch of the Sackville family) as well as a memorial to Vita Sackville-West - the poet and owner of Sissinghurst Castle in Kent who died in 1962.

BURWASH

Standing on a hill which is surrounded by land that is marsh for part of the year, Burwash is an exceptionally pretty village with a high street that is chiefly lined with charming 17TH and 18TH century timber framed cottages. Among the buildings found here is **Rampyndene** - a handsome house with a sweeping roof that was built in 1699 for a wealthy local timber merchant. Burwash was a major centre of the Wealden iron industry between the 15th and 17th centuries and this brought much prosperity to the village.

However, it is not the village that brings most people to Burwash (though it certainly deserves the attention), but a house just outside. In 1902, Rudyard Kipling moved from Rottingdean to **Bateman's** to combat the growing

problem of over enthusiastic sightseers. Located down a steep and narrow lane, the Jacobean house was originally built in 1634 for a prosperous local ironmaster and combined with its surrounding 33 acres of beautiful grounds - landscaped by Kipling and his wife to complement the house - it proved the perfect retreat.

Kipling and his wife lived here until their deaths - he in 1936 and she just three years later - and during his time here the author wrote many of his famous works including *Puck of Pook's Corner*, *If* and the Sussex poems. Now in the hands of the National Trust, the house has been left as it was when the Kiplings lived here and among the personal items on display is a watercolour of Rudyard Lake in Staffordshire- the place where his parents met and which they nostalgically remembered at the time of their son's birth out in Bombay. Also here, are a series of terracotta plaques that were designed by Kipling's father, Lockwood Kipling, and used to illustrate his novel *Kim*. Lockwood was an architectural sculptor and went to India as the principal of an art school; he later became the curator of Lahore Museum.

THE ROSE & CROWN

Ham Lane, Burwash, East Sussex TN19 7ER
Tel/Fax: 01435 882600
e-mail: info@roseandcrownburwash.co.uk
website: www.roseandcrownburwash.co.uk

Good appetizing food, fine, quality wines, cask conditioned Sussex ales, comfortable accommodation and a warm, friendly welcome from licencees Ted and Maggie Hirst all await visitors who find their way to **The Rose & Crown**. Located in the pretty and charismatic village of Burwash, this well-built, roomy village inn dates back to the 15th Century and its low doorways, small paned windows and prominent brick chimneys betray its past.

As well as being popular with the locals and passing trade, the pub is also home to two resident ghosts – the white lady who haunts the landing and her fellow spectre who prefers to inhabit the

inglenook fireplace in the bar! For à la carte dining or private functions, the pub has an excellent restaurant which is just the ticket. For more casual dining, bar meals can be enjoyed in the main bar, at the picnic benches on the cobbled forecourt or in the rear patio garden which is a perfect spot for eating al fresco.

Occasionally on Saturday evenings there's some live music, but if you are a folk and blues lover, it's worth remembering that there's a regular Sunday evening session throughout the year.

Whilst here the Kipling's only son, John was killed on active duty during World War I at Loos, France in 1915. There is a tablet to the 18 year old in the village church.

AROUND BURWASH

THREE LEG CROSS
4 miles N of Burwash off the B2099

In 1975, the Southern Water Authority dammed the River Bewl to create **Bewl Bridge Reservoir** - the largest area of inland water in the southeast of England. A great many buildings were lost under the water but one, the 15TH century **Dunsters Mill**, was taken down brick by brick before the waters rose, and placed above the high

water level. Another couple of timber framed farm buildings in the valley also found themselves uprooted and transported to the Weald and Downland Museum at Singleton.

More than just a reservoir, the land around Bewl Bridge is a Country Park and has much to offer including lakeside walks, trout fishing, pleasure boat trips and glorious countryside.

TICEHURST
3½ N of Burwash on the B2099

This ancient village is filled with attractive tile hung and white weather boarded buildings that are so characteristic of the settlements along the Sussex and Kent border. Among the particularly noteworthy buildings here are **Furze**

House - a former workhouse, and **Whatman's** - an old carpenter's cottage with strangely curving walls. The village is also home to **Pashley Manor Gardens**, which surround the 16th century Grade I listed timber frame house. With waterfalls, ponds and a moat, these romantic gardens are typically English. Less formally, there is a woodland area and a chain of ponds that are surrounded by rhododendrons, azaleas and climbing roses. The gardens and house are privately owned but the gardens are open to the public on a limited basis.

ETCHINGHAM
2 miles NE of Burwash on the A265

This scattered settlement, found in the broad lush valley of the River Rother, was home to the fortified manor of the de Echyngham family in the Middle Ages. Built to protect a crossing point on the River Rother, the house has long since gone and has since been replaced by the village commuter station. Just outside the village lies **Haremere Hall** - an impressive 17TH century manor house that is now a centre for Shire horses. Several breeds of heavy horse are bred and trained here, including Shires, Clydesdales, Suffolk Punches and Ardennes and the combination of their sheer power and docility needs to be experienced at first hand to be fully appreciated.

BRIGHTLING
2½ miles S of Burwash off the B2096

The character of this tiny hillside village is completely overshadowed by the character of one of its former residents. It is certainly not unkind to say that the Georgian eccentric, 'Mad' Jack Fuller, was larger than life since he weighed some 22 stones and was affectionately referred to as the 'Hippopotamus'! A local ironmaster,

squire and generous philanthropist, 'Mad' Jack also sat as an MP for East Sussex between 1801 and 1812, but was only elected after a campaign that cost him and his supporters a massive £50,000. Fuller was one of the first people to recognise the talents of a young painter, JMW Turner, and he was also responsible for saving Bodiam Castle from ruin.

However, it is for his series of imaginative follies that this colourful character is best remembered. He commissioned many of the buildings to provide work for his foundry employees during the decline of the iron industry, and among those that remain today are Brightling Observatory - now a private house, a Rotunda Temple on his estate and the **Brightling Needle**. The 40 foot stone obelisk was built on a rise to the north of the village which is itself, 650 feet above sea level.

One of Fuller's more eccentric buildings was the result of a wager. Having bet with a friend on the number of spires that were visible from his home, Brightling Park, Fuller arrived back to find that in fact the steeple of Dallington church was not visible. In order to win the bet, Fuller quickly ordered his men to erect a 35 foot mock spire in a meadow on a direct line with Dallington, and the monument is affectionately referred to as the **Sugar Loaf**. Perhaps, though, Fuller's greatest structure is his 25 foot pyramid mausoleum which he built in the parish churchyard some 24 years before his death. When he died, the story went around that he was buried inside in a sitting position, wearing a top hat and holding a bottle of claret. However, despite the appropriateness of this image of his life, the parish church quashed the idea by stating that he was buried in the normal, horizontal pose.

HERSTMONCEUX
8 miles S of Burwash on the A271

The village is famous as being the home of **Herstmonceux Castle** which was built on the site of an early Norman manor house in 1440 by Sir Roger Fiennes. A remarkable building on two counts: it was one of the first large scale buildings in the country to be built of brick and it was also one of the first castles to combine the need for security with the

Herstmonceux Castle

comforts of the residents. As the castle was built on a lake there was added protection and the impressive gatehouse, with its murder holes and arrow slits, presented an aggressive front to any would be attackers.

Later, the castle passed into the hands of the Hare family, who presided over a long period of decline for Herstmonceux which culminated in most of the interior being stripped to provide building materials for another house in 1777. The castle sadly lay semi derelict for 150 years before a major programme of restoration was undertaken in the 1930s under the supervision of a Lewes architect, WH Godfrey. His careful and inspired work saw the turrets and battlements returned to their former romantic glory, and today the castle is as pristine as it was when it was first built.

In 1948, the Royal Observatory at Greenwich was looking for somewhere to move to away from the glow of the street lights of London. It was moved to Herstmonceux, and after 20 careful years of planning and building, they opened the gigantic Isaac Newton telescope in the grounds. One of the five largest in the world, it was officially opened in 1967. In 1989, the Royal Observatory moved again

leaving the castle to become a conference centre. The castle is also home to the **Herstmonceux Science Centre** where, among the domes and telescopes that the astronomers used between the 1950s and the 1980s, visitors can experience the wonder of viewing the heavens. There are also hands on displays and an Astronomy Exhibition which traces the history and work of the world famous Observatory.

Though the castle is not open to the public, **Herstmonceux Castle Garden** - the 500 acres of Elizabethan grounds around the splendid moated castle are open for most the year. In the formal section of the grounds is a 16th century walled garden, a herb garden, the waterlily filled moat and a Georgian style folly. Walks in the woodland area will take you to the remains of the 300 year old sweet chestnut avenue and the intermittent waterfall.

HORAM
8 miles SW of Burwash on the A267

Situated beside the main road is a large cider press which at first seems strange in Sussex but was placed there by the makers of Merrydown cider when they came to the village in the 1940s.

WARBLETON
6 miles SW of Burwash off the B2203

Found amongst a series of crisscrossing lanes, the village is little more than its church and a handful of houses. Inside the church is a magnificent galleried pew dating from the 18TH century that has two compartments on a level with the first floor. Whether these were used for checking the church attendance or for dozing off in during a dreary sermon no one is quite sure.

CROSS IN HAND
8 miles W of Burwash on the A267

This intriguingly named settlement lies on a busy road junction that has a post mill standing in the triangle formed by the converging roads. Certainly worth a second glance, the windmill at one time stood five miles away at Uckfield.

HEATHFIELD
6 miles W of Burwash on the A265

To the east of the town centre lies the large expanse of **Heathfield Park**, once owned by General Sir George Augustus Elliot (later Lord Heathfield), the Governor of Gibraltar and commander of the British garrison that successfully withstood attacks from both France and Spain between 1779 and 1782. Despite the wall surrounding the grounds, **Gibraltar Tower** - a castellated folly erected on his estate in his honour, can be seen.

Heathfield remained a quiet and undistinguished town until the arrival of the Tunbridge Wells to Eastbourne railway in the 19TH century. It then grew to become an important market town for the local area.

The **Cuckoo Trail** is a 25km, traffic free trail following the track of an old railway

THE CROSS IN HAND INN

Cross in Hand, near Heathfield, East Sussex TN21 0SN
Tel: 01435 862053

The Cross in Hand is a part timbered, part boarded public house and restaurant set in the curious village that gives the pub its name. Exposed oak beams and wood panelling reveal that the building dates back in parts to the 15th century. Congenial and conscientious proprietors, Mo and Jackie Chatfield have taken great care and attention when renovating this welcoming establishment to ensure that the original character and feeling is retained. The fine selection of real ales on offer can be imbibed in front of a roaring log fire in winter, or outside in the tranquil beer garden on warmer days.

A very substantial English breakfast with all the trimmings including sausages, eggs, bacon, black pudding, mushrooms and toast washed down with tea or coffee is served daily. A broad selection of

appetising lunches, bar snacks and evening meals is also available seven days a week, and the sumptuous traditional Sunday lunch is guaranteed to keep you going for the rest of the day. Guests can choose to eat in the non smoking restaurant overlooking the garden if they prefer. Pensioners perks and a smaller portions, smaller prices policy means that the reasonably priced menus cater to suit all purses making this a busy destination, so it's best to book in advance to guarantee a seat.

linking Heathfield with Eastbourne. Perfect for walking, cycling and horse riding, the route also acts as a make shift gallery with art designed by local artists along the way.

MAYFIELD
6 miles NW of Burwash off the A267

This ancient settlement possesses one of the finest main streets in East Sussex and is one of the most picturesque villages in the area. According to local legend, St Dunstan, a skilled blacksmith by trade, stopped here in the 10TH century to preach Christianity to the pagan people of this remote Wealden community. Whilst working at his anvil, St Dunstan was confronted by the Devil disguised as a beautiful maiden, who attempted to seduce the missionary. However, St Dunstan spotted that the feet of his young temptress were cloven, and recognising her as Satan, grabbed her by the nose with a pair of red hot tongs. The Devil let out an almighty scream and beat a hasty retreat; but he was soon to return, this time dressed as a traveller in need of new shoes for his horse. Dunstan again saw through the deception and, threatening Satan with his blacksmith's tools, forced him to promise never again to enter a

Windmill, Mayfield

house which had a horseshoe above the door.

St Dunstan went on to become the Archbishop of Canterbury in 959, and some time later, **Mayfield Palace** - one of the great residences of the medieval Archbishops of Canterbury was built here. Though little remains of the grand palace now, a Roman Catholic Convent School incorporates the surviving buildings. Also whilst he was living here, St Dunstan founded a simple timber church that was replaced by a stone structure in the 13TH century. After a fire and being struck by

Mayfield

lightning, the present day church of St Dunstan is now a conglomeration of styles. Inside is a Jacobean pulpit, a font dated 1666 and some impressive 17TH and 18TH century monuments to the Baker family

WADHURST
5 miles NW of Burwash on the B2099

This was another great centre of the Wealden iron industry in the 17TH and 18TH centuries and was also one of the last places in Sussex to hold out against the improved coal fired smelting techniques which had taken root in the north. Though the village **Church of St Peter and St Paul** is not quite built of iron, the floor is almost entirely made up of iron tomb slabs - a unique collection which marks the graves of local ironmasters who died between 1617 and 1772.

The village was dominated by iron and many of Wadhurst's fine buildings date from the industry's heyday, including the large Queen Anne vicarage, on the High Street, that was built by John Legas, the town's chief ironmaster. In the late 19TH century, the village sought fame when important prize fights were held here with many of the spectators travelling from London to this rather obscure venue by train.

Bewl Water, the south east's largest lake, offers the visitor plenty of pretty woodland walks and picnic areas, plus at Lamberhurst there's an interesting visitors' centre and interactive exhibition, and various other leisure facilities

Situated in the picturesque wooded valley of the River Teise and owned by English Heritage, **Bayham Abbey** is an impressive sandstone building constructed in the 13th century, and a popular location for painters and photographers. Amongst the surviving remains are the church, claustral buildings and gatehouse. The Georgian Dower House is also open to view.

List of Tourist Information Centres

EAST SUSSEX

ASHDOWN FOREST LLAMA PARK
Wych Cross
Forest Row
East Sussex
RH18 5JN
Tel: 01825 713862
Fax: 01825 713812
e-mail: ticnorth@wealden.gov.uk

BATTLE
88 High Street
Battle
East Sussex
TN33 0AQ
Tel: 01424 773721
Fax: 01424 773436
e-mail: battletic@rother.gov.uk

BEXHILL-ON-SEA
51 Marina
Bexhill-on-Sea
East Sussex
TN40 1BQ
Tel: 01424 732208
Fax: 01424 212500
e-mail: bexhilltic@rother.gov.uk

BOSHIP ROUNDABOUT A22
Lower Dicker
Hailsham
East Sussex
BN27 4DT
Tel: 01323 442667
Fax: 01323 449584
e-mail: sussexcountry.tic@wealden.gov.uk

BRIGHTON
10 Bartholomew Square
Brighton
East Sussex
BN1 1JS
Fax: 01273 292594
e-mail: brighton-tourism@brighton-hove.gov.uk

EASTBOURNE
Cornfield Road
Eastbourne
East Sussex
BN21 4QL
Tel: 01323 411400
Fax: 01323 649574
e-mail: eastbournetic@btclick.com

HASTINGS
Queens Square
Priory Meadow
Hastings
East Sussex
TN34 1TL
Tel: 01424 781111
Fax: 01424 781186
e-mail: hic_info@hastings.gov.uk

HASTINGS
The Stade
Old Town
Hastings
East Sussex
TN34 1EZ
Tel: 01424 781111
Fax: 01424 781186
e-mail: hic_info@hastings.gov.uk

HOVE
Church Road
Hove
East Sussex
BN3 3BQ
Tel: 01273 292589

LEWES
187 High Street
Lewes
East Sussex
BN7 2DE
Tel: 01273 483448
Fax: 01273 484003
e-mail: lewestic@lewes.gov.uk

RYE
The Heritage Centre,
Strand Quay
Rye
East Sussex
TN31 7AY
Tel: 01797 226696
Fax: 01797 223460
e-mail: ryetic@rother.gov.uk

SEAFORD
25 Clinton Place
Seafoird
East Sussex
BN25 1NP
Tel/Fax: 01323 897426
e-mail: seafordtic@lewes.gov.uk

WEST SUSSEX

ARUNDEL

61 High Street
Arundel
West Sussex
BN18 9AJ
Tel: 01903 882268
Fax: 01903 882419
e-mail: tourism@arun.gov.uk
website: http://www.sussexbythesea.com/

BOGNOR REGIS

Belmont Street
Bognor Regis
West Sussex
PO21 1BJ
Tel: 01243 823140
Fax: 01243 820435
e-mail: tourism@arun.gov.uk
website: http://www.sussexbythesea.com/

BURGESS HILL

96 Church Walk
Burgess Hill
West Sussex
RH15 9AS
Tel: 01444 247726
Fax: 01444 233707
e-mail: touristinformation@burgesshill.gov.uk

CHICHESTER

29a South Street
Chichester
West Sussex
PO19 1AH
Tel: 01243 775888
Fax: 01243 539449
e-mail: Chitic@chichester.gov.uk

HORSHAM

9 The Causeway
Horsham
West Sussex
RH12 1HE
Tel: 01403 211661
Fax: 01403 217581
e-mail: touristinformation@horsham.gov.uk

LITTLEHAMPTON

Windmill Complex
Littlehampton
West Sussex
BN17 5LH
Tel: 01903 713480
Fax: 01903 713480
e-mail: tourism@arun.gov.uk
website: http://www.sussexbythesea.com/

MIDHURST

North Street
Midhurst
West Sussex
GU29 9DW
Tel: 01730 817322
Fax: 01730 817120

PETWORTH

Market Square
Petworth
West Sussex
GU28 0AF
Tel: 01798 343523
Fax: 01798 343942

WORTHING

Chapel Road
Worthing
West Sussex
BN11 1HL
Tel: 01903 210022
Fax: 01903 236277
e-mail: wbctourism@pavilion.co.uk

Index of Towns, Villages and Places of Interest

List of Advertisers

Hidden Places Order Form

To order any of our publications just fill in the payment details below and complete the order form *overleaf*. For orders of less than 4 copies please add £1 per book for postage and packing. Orders over 4 copies are P & P free.

Please Complete Either:

I enclose a cheque for £ [   ] made payable to Travel Publishing Ltd

Or:

Card No: [   ]

Expiry Date: [   ]

Signature: [   ]

NAME: [   ]

ADDRESS: [   ]

POSTCODE: [   ]

TEL NO: [   ]

Please either send, telephone or e-mail your order to:

Travel Publishing Ltd, 7a Apollo House, Calleva Park, Aldermaston, Berkshire RG7 8TN
Tel: 0118 981 7777   Fax: 0118 982 0077
e-mail: karen@travelpublishing.co.uk
website: www.travelpublishing.co.uk

	PRICE	QUANTITY	VALUE

HIDDEN PLACES REGIONAL TITLES

	PRICE	QUANTITY	VALUE
Cambs & Lincolnshire	£7.99	....	....
Chilterns	£8.99	....	....
Cornwall	£8.99	....	....
Derbyshire	£8.99	....	....
Devon	£8.99	....	....
Dorset, Hants & Isle of Wight	£8.99	....	....
East Anglia	£8.99	....	....
Gloucs, Wiltshire & Somerset	£8.99	....	....
Heart of England	£7.99	....	....
Hereford, Worcs & Shropshire	£7.99	....	....
Highlands & Islands	£7.99	....	....
Kent	£8.99	....	....
Lake District & Cumbria	£8.99	....	....
Lancashire & Cheshire	£8.99	....	....
Lincolnshire & Nottinghamshire	£8.99	....	....
Northumberland & Durham	£8.99	....	....
Sussex	£8.99	....	....
Thames Valley	£7.99	....	....
Yorkshire	£8.99	....	....

HIDDEN PLACES NATIONAL TITLES

	PRICE	QUANTITY	VALUE
England	£9.99	....	....
Ireland	£9.99	....	....
Scotland	£9.99	....	....
Wales	£9.99	....	....

HIDDEN INNS TITLES

	PRICE	QUANTITY	VALUE
East Anglia	£5.99	....	....
Heart of England	£5.99	....	....
Lancashire & Cheshire	£5.99	....	....
South	£5.99	....	....
South East	£5.99	....	....
South and Central Scotland	£5.99	....	....
North of England	£5.99	....	....
Wales	£5.99	....	....
Welsh Borders	£5.99	....	....
West Country	£5.99	....	....
Yorkshire	£5.99	....	....

For orders of less than 4 copies please add £1 per book for postage & packing. Orders over 4 copies P & P free.

Hidden Places Order Form

To order any of our publications just fill in the payment details below and complete the order form *overleaf*. For orders of less than 4 copies please add £1 per book for postage and packing. Orders over 4 copies are P & P free.

Please Complete Either:

I enclose a cheque for £ [ ] made payable to Travel Publishing Ltd

Or:

Card No: [ ]

Expiry Date: [ ]

Signature: [ ]

NAME: [ ]

ADDRESS: [ ]

POSTCODE: [ ]

TEL NO: [ ]

Please either send, telephone or e-mail your order to:

Travel Publishing Ltd, 7a Apollo House, Calleva Park, Aldermaston, Berkshire RG7 8TN
Tel: 0118 981 7777   Fax: 0118 982 0077
e-mail: karen@travelpublishing.co.uk
website: www.travelpublishing.co.uk

	PRICE	QUANTITY	VALUE

HIDDEN PLACES REGIONAL TITLES

	PRICE	QUANTITY	VALUE
Cambs & Lincolnshire	£7.99	....	....
Chilterns	£8.99	....	....
Cornwall	£8.99	....	....
Derbyshire	£8.99	....	....
Devon	£8.99	....	....
Dorset, Hants & Isle of Wight	£8.99	....	....
East Anglia	£8.99	....	....
Gloucs, Wiltshire & Somerset	£8.99	....	....
Heart of England	£7.99	....	....
Hereford, Worcs & Shropshire	£7.99	....	....
Highlands & Islands	£7.99	....	....
Kent	£8.99	....	....
Lake District & Cumbria	£8.99	....	....
Lancashire & Cheshire	£8.99	....	....
Lincolnshire & Nottinghamshire	£8.99	....	....
Northumberland & Durham	£8.99	....	....
Sussex	£8.99	....	....
Thames Valley	£7.99	....	....
Yorkshire	£8.99	....	....

HIDDEN PLACES NATIONAL TITLES

	PRICE	QUANTITY	VALUE
England	£9.99	....	....
Ireland	£9.99	....	....
Scotland	£9.99	....	....
Wales	£9.99	....	....

HIDDEN INNS TITLES

	PRICE	QUANTITY	VALUE
East Anglia	£5.99	....	....
Heart of England	£5.99	....	....
Lancashire & Cheshire	£5.99	....	....
South	£5.99	....	....
South East	£5.99	....	....
South and Central Scotland	£5.99	....	....
North of England	£5.99	....	....
Wales	£5.99	....	....
Welsh Borders	£5.99	....	....
West Country	£5.99	....	....
Yorkshire	£5.99	....	....

For orders of less than 4 copies please add £1 per book for postage & packing. Orders over 4 copies P & P free.

Hidden Places Reader Reaction

The *Hidden Places* research team would like to receive reader's comments on any visitor attractions or places reviewed in the book and also recommendations for suitable entries to be included in the next edition. This will help ensure that the *Hidden Places* series continues to provide its readers with useful information on the more interesting, unusual or unique features of each attraction or place ensuring that their stay in the local area is an enjoyable and stimulating experience. To provide your comments or recommendations would you please complete the forms below and overleaf as indicated and send to:

The Research Department, Travel Publishing Ltd,
7a Apollo House, Calleva Park, Aldermaston, Reading, RG7 8TN.

Your Name:

Your Address:

Your Telephone Number:

Please tick as appropriate: Comments ☐   Recommendation ☐

Name of *"Hidden Place"*:

Address:

Telephone Number:

Name of Contact:

Hidden Places Reader Reaction

Comment or Reason for Recommendation:

Hidden Places Reader Reaction

The *Hidden Places* research team would like to receive reader's comments on any visitor attractions or places reviewed in the book and also recommendations for suitable entries to be included in the next edition. This will help ensure that the *Hidden Places* series continues to provide its readers with useful information on the more interesting, unusual or unique features of each attraction or place ensuring that their stay in the local area is an enjoyable and stimulating experience. To provide your comments or recommendations would you please complete the forms below and overleaf as indicated and send to:

The Research Department, Travel Publishing Ltd,

7a Apollo House, Calleva Park, Aldermaston, Reading, RG7 8TN.

Your Name:

Your Address:

Your Telephone Number:

Please tick as appropriate: Comments ☐   Recommendation ☐

Name of *"Hidden Place"*:

Address:

Telephone Number:

Name of Contact:

Hidden Places Reader Reaction

Comment or Reason for Recommendation:

....

....

....

....

....

....

....

....

....

....

....

Hidden Places Reader Reaction

The *Hidden Places* research team would like to receive reader's comments on any visitor attractions or places reviewed in the book and also recommendations for suitable entries to be included in the next edition. This will help ensure that the *Hidden Places* series continues to provide its readers with useful information on the more interesting, unusual or unique features of each attraction or place ensuring that their stay in the local area is an enjoyable and stimulating experience. To provide your comments or recommendations would you please complete the forms below and overleaf as indicated and send to:

The Research Department, Travel Publishing Ltd,
7a Apollo House, Calleva Park, Aldermaston, Reading, RG7 8TN.

Your Name:

Your Address:

Your Telephone Number:

Please tick as appropriate: Comments ☐ Recommendation ☐

Name of *"Hidden Place"*:

Address:

Telephone Number:

Name of Contact:

Hidden Places Reader Reaction

Comment or Reason for Recommendation:

....

....

....

....

....

....

....

....

....

....